EASY PIANO

Country Songs
FOR KIDS

ISBN 978-1-70513-747-5

Visit Hal Leonard Online at
www.halleonard.com

Contact us:
Hal Leonard
7777 West Bluemound Road
Milwaukee, WI 53213
Email: info@halleonard.com

In Europe, contact:
Hal Leonard Europe Limited
42 Wigmore Street
Marylebone, London, W1U 2RN
Email: info@halleonardeurope.com

In Australia, contact:
Hal Leonard Australia Pty. Ltd.
4 Lentara Court
Cheltenham, Victoria, 3192 Australia
Email: info@halleonard.com.au

Contents

Song Notes

ACHY BREAKY HEART
(Don't Tell My Heart)

Recorded in 1991 by Billy Ray Cyrus on his debut album, "Achy Breaky Heart" became a hit on both the country and popular charts. It became Cyrus' signature song and was very popular as a country line dance. Head out to the dance floor, but first notice that this arrangement is written in the key of G major. It uses only two chords: G and D, making the left-hand part extremely easy to play. There are two patterns for left hand: G-D for the G chord, and D-A for the D chord. Play the right-hand eighth notes with a relaxed feel and a bit of swing.

AMAZED

This amazingly popular power ballad was #1 on both Billboard's country chart and the Hot 100 in 2000. Sung by Lonestar, it's the group's biggest hit. Play the opening in a lyrical style, smooth and connected, noting the moderately slow tempo indication. Start to build in intensity as you play into the 2nd ending at bar 27 and continue through the repeat of the chorus. Observe the *ritard* and *decrescendo* sign in the last two measures, bringing the song to a quiet, gentle ending.

BE A LIGHT

Known for his personal and nostalgic songs, Thomas Rhett brought together fellow country stars Reba McEntire, Hillary Scott, Chris Tomlin, and Keith Urban to record "Be a Light" during the coronavirus outbreak in 2020. Proceeds from this uplifting ballad were donated to the MusiCares COVID-19 Relief Fund. Organized by a simple left-hand bass line: A-B-C, this repetition gives structure to the verses. Play in a gentle and steady style, highlighting the lyrics, with the message of hope and encouragement.

BLESS THE BROKEN ROAD

Along the road to finding true love there are many lessons learned, and this song is about that journey, and has been recorded by several country music artists. The most well-known version, sung by the group Rascal Flatts in 2004, won a GRAMMY® Award for Best Country Song. Choose a moderate tempo and use the lyrics to help you lean into the gentle syncopation. The rhythm eighth note-quarter note-eighth note appears throughout the song. Look for patterns in the melody, like the leap of a 4th (G-C) that begins many two-measure phrases, and the pick-up notes leading to beat one throughout the chorus: E-F-G, starting in bar 25. Enjoy the keyboard solo after the first chorus (bars 45–51) and in the coda (bar 74 to the end).

COAT OF MANY COLORS

—◇—

"Coat of Many Colors" is a song written and recorded in 1971 by Dolly Parton. It tells the story of the coat Dolly's mother made for her from rags, comparing it to the coat Joseph wore in the biblical story of his "coat of many colors." Dolly was delighted with the coat and excited to wear it but was laughed at for wearing a coat made of rags. But there's more. Play this song to learn the rest of the story. The simply constructed melody lets you concentrate on the lyrics, and the bass line stays within a small span, creating a firm foundation. Notice a little "walking" bass pattern in bar 12: B♭-A-G-F leading you down to the keynote, F. As you descend the notes step by step, your fingers are "walking" from note to note. Slightly emphasize this walking bass line whenever it occurs.

CRAZY

—◇—

Written in 1961 by Willie Nelson, this classic country ballad was recorded by many artists, most notably by Patsy Cline. With a melody that twists and turns and some beautiful, jazz-like harmony, this song will have you humming along as you learn it. Look at the right-hand melody. Right away you'll notice the quarter-note triplets, written as three quarter notes under a bracket. These three notes take the time of two beats. As you play them against the half notes in the left hand, stretch the three notes, giving them each one third of those two beats. It takes a bit of careful listening, but you'll soon have a feel for it. If you like, listen to an original recording by Patsy Cline, or even Willie Nelson himself, to hear examples. The left-hand part includes quite a few accidentals (sharps and flats not in the key signature) which give the song it's jazzy feel.

THE DEVIL WENT DOWN TO GEORGIA

—◇—

The Charlie Daniels Band's biggest hit, this lively 1979 bluegrass tune is full of fun. You don't have to make a deal with the devil to learn this classic, but slow practice and attention to fingering will make it easier to play. Those sixteenth-note passages in the introduction and inserted throughout were originally played by the fiddle, so keep the feeling light and articulate each note cleanly. The verses are uniquely performed in a somewhat spoken style. You begin in the key of D minor but watch out for the key change to D major at bar 77, exchanging one flat for two sharps. Sixteen bars later you're back to D minor as the story continues and ends with a dramatic flourish.

FOREVER AND EVER, AMEN

—◇—

This sweet country love song was recorded by Randy Travis in 1987 and won a GRAMMY for Best Country & Western Song in 1988. Simply constructed, notice that left hand alternates between D and G for the first 12 bars, followed by E7 and A7. This pattern continues for the rest of the song, until a little variation in the last eight bars. The fermata signs ⌒ in the last line mean to hold the note or notes below them for longer than the written value. It's the performer's choice on how long to hold a fermata.

THE GAMBLER

Kenny Roger's biggest hit and signature song, this country classic was released in 1976 and is set on a train "bound for nowhere." Telling the story of a gambler down on his luck, the narrator sings one of country music's most remembered refrains, which begins with, "You got to know when to hold 'em, know when to fold 'em, know when to walk away, and know when to run." But before the refrain, check out the verses that tell this story. Beginning with the first bar, right hand plays up-stemmed melody notes, and down-stemmed harmony notes. Play the melody strongly, but play the down-stemmed notes more quietly, balancing the sound so melody is prominent. Left hand plays a one-note bass line, making it easy for you to concentrate on the melody.

GOD BLESS THE U.S.A.

Considered a signature song for Lee Greenwood, this patriotic country hit was first performed in 1984 and has been re-recorded several times since. Choose a tempo that allows you to let the lyrics shine, but don't let it drag. The quarter note gets the beat. Based on that, think about the speed of the opening eighth notes before you play the sixteenth-note pick-ups. It's easy to rush this song, so a relaxed feel is best. At the chorus, keep a gentle feel for the dotted sixteenths. They will flow along with the lyrics, and don't need extra emphasis. Take some time with the *ritard* in the last two bars, slowing into the last few beats. If the 7ths are hard to reach for your hand size, playing just the lowest notes will work well too.

GRANDPA
(Tell Me 'Bout the Good Old Days)

Performed by the mother-daughter duo The Judds in 1986, this tune is about longing for simpler times. And as for the harmony, that's simple too! You'll need to learn just three chords: B♭, F and C7. A Gm7 chord sneaks in at the end of the song for a little color. Note the left-hand patterns, and the way it "walks" up and down the bass notes, sometimes called a "walking" bass. You'll see this right away in the left-hand pick-up notes, again in bar 4 (walking down), bar 10 (walking up) and bar 16 (walking down). Look through the rest of the song and you'll see these patterns repeat.

GREEN GREEN GRASS OF HOME

Written by Claude "Curly" Putman Jr. and performed most famously in 1965 by Porter Wagoner, "Green Green Grass of Home" tells a story that has an unexpected ending. Choose a moderately slow tempo to highlight the lyrics and play the poignant melody in a *legato* style. The left-hand part never reaches beyond an octave, so left-hand fifth finger on the low G will keep you anchored. Follow the repeat signs and ending brackets to guide you through all the verses.

THE HOUSE THAT BUILT ME

———◇———

Miranda Lambert recorded this country ballad, which tells the story of growing up and treasuring family memories, in 2010. The tempo "Moderately fast, in 2" indicates a feeling of forward movement, thinking in two beats per bar, rather than four. When you play through this song the first time, count through the right-hand rhythms carefully. There's lots of syncopation, but also lots of repetition. Once you have the feel for it, it's easy. The harmony played by the left hand uses F, C, and B♭ major chords, often four bars at a time. Am, Dm, and Gm7 bring a bit of color to the story later in the song, but the left hand stays pretty much in the same place throughout.

I HOPE YOU DANCE

———◇———

"I Hope You Dance" was a big hit for Lee Ann Womack, becoming her signature song. Released in 2000, it won multiple awards including the Country Music Association's Single of the Year and a GRAMMY for best country song. To showcase its country-pop feel and uplifting message, learn the syncopated right-hand melody carefully. There's a lot of syncopation (accents and emphasis on unexpected, or weak beats) throughout the verse. Play slowly the first few times, counting steady eighth notes through the ties. The simple left-hand accompaniment allows you to let the melody shine.

I WALK THE LINE

———◇———

Johnny Cash had his first #1 hit with this song in 1956. He performed it frequently during his career and re-recorded it four times. The distinctive chord progression makes use of a walking bass between the C and F chords. Examples of this include the left hand in bars 6–7, and 8–9. The left hand "walks" up: C-D-E-F, and then walks down: F-E-D-C. In bars 12–13 the entire measure walks down from F to B♭. Whenever you can, emphasize this bass line, but don't overdo it! You'll want the melody to sing out as the lyrics tell this classic story of personal responsibility, making good choices, and avoiding temptation.

KEEP ON THE SUNNY SIDE

———◇———

This cheerful country tune was recorded by The Carter Family in 1928. They continued to perform the song throughout their career, making it a theme song of sorts. With a very simple rhythm and just a few chords, you'll be singing along right away. Follow the repeat sign to sing through verses 1–2, but after the third verse, take the third ending, directing you to *D.S. al Coda*, which means go back to the sign 𝄋 on the previous page for a repeat of the chorus. At the end of bar 30 you'll see To Coda ⊕ which directs you to the coda at bar 35. Practice reading through this "road map" of the form before you play.

LOVE ME TENDER

———◇———

You may recognize the melody of this Elvis Presley 1956 hit as the civil war ballad "Aura Lee." Popular with glee clubs and barbershop quartets, Presley adapted the melody and new lyrics were added. Play this sweet song with a beautiful, singing tone and a well-balanced left hand. Especially note the harmonic movement in bars 11–14. The chromatic accidentals in the bass clef give the harmony a bit of color through the last phrase.

MAY THE BIRD OF PARADISE
FLY UP YOUR NOSE

———◇———

This country novelty song first performed by "Little" Jimmy Dickens in 1965 has a quirky title and is said to have been inspired by late-night host Johnny Carson. Each verse is a humorous insult, wishing the recipient the bad luck of having the very large bird of paradise fly (as if it could!) up their nose. Have a little fun as you play this up-tempo number! Lean into the distinctive syncopation in the verse (eighth note-quarter note) and in the chorus (eighth note tied into the quarter note of the following measure).

MOST PEOPLE ARE GOOD

———◇———

Luke Bryan sings this 2018 contemporary country song with a relaxed, uplifting vibe. Check out the left-hand part to note a repeating bass line pattern. Count through the right-hand melody as you play it the first time. There's a good amount of syncopation (usually accents on the "and" of the beat) so get comfortable leaning into those tied notes and eighth note-quarter note-eighth note rhythms. Sing along with the melody—you'll enjoy its feel-good message.

RAINBOW

———◇———

This lyrical piano ballad first performed by Kacey Musgraves in 2018 is the perfect song for the "rainy" or dark times in our lives. Take your time with this beautiful melody and message of hope, being careful not to rush the tempo. Set a strong quarter-note pulse and let the lyrics guide you into a bit of *rubato* (a push and pull of the tempo) but be sure to play the tied notes for their full value. Enjoy the chord changes, listening for a full, round tone as you sink into the keys.

RING OF FIRE

—◇—

This classic tune was one of Johnny Cash's biggest hits, holding on to the #1 spot on the country charts for seven weeks in 1963. You won't need to fall into a burning ring of fire to have fun playing this song! On the recording the song opens with the sound of mariachi horns, and here we have that melody played by the right hand. The verse stays in a very narrow range, but the left-hand accompaniment spans an octave. Practice left hand alone to get a feel for the octave distance in the repeating pattern using this fingering starting in bar 3: 3-1-5-1. Don't look down at your hand while playing, but rather, trust how the distance between the keys feels once you've learned the pattern.

SIMPLE

—◇—

Keeping things simple in love and relationships is the message of this 2018 Florida Georgia Line hit. The introduction mimic's the opening whistle on the recording, along with a spare left-hand accompaniment written with half and whole notes. Play this song in 2, a feel of two beats per measure, to make the most of its upbeat tempo, and have fun with the lyrics, you'll be spelling out the song title before you're done.

SIXTEEN TONS

—◇—

Tennessee Ernie Ford recorded this famous song about life in the coal mines in 1946. It was #1 on both the country and pop charts, and later sung by dozens of artists, including Johnny Cash, Elvis Presley, and the Weavers. Check out the syncopation in the opening measures. This distinctive rhythm, with the "and" of beat 2 tied into beat 3 appears throughout the song. Play the melody with a bit of swing, as indicated at the beginning of the song with this symbol: (♫ = ♩♪) and really slow it down for a dramatic ending. The term *molto rit.* means "much slower."

STUCK LIKE GLUE

—◇—

This 2010, quirky but happy song about two sweethearts "stuck like glue" is performed by the country duo Sugarland. With a three-chord pattern, D-A-G (with Em sneaking in a couple of times) you'll find this arrangement easy to learn. Once you've discovered this, don't hold back on a bouncy tempo, and be sure to "swing" the eighth notes for a "long-short" feel as indicated by (♫ = ♩♪) at the beginning of the song, next to the tempo designation.

WIDE OPEN SPACES

—◇—

This popular tune tells the story of a daughter leaving home, following a dream, seeking adventure and independence. The Chicks first performed this song in 1998 and its bluegrass feel highlights fiddle, mandolin, and banjo on the recording. Look at the left-hand part in bars 5–8. You'll see that rhythm repeated throughout as an accompaniment pattern. Even when the notes change, the rhythm stays the same. At the chorus (bar 20) left-hand rhythm switches to repeated quarter notes, so let that motion propel you through to the instrumental break at bar 31. One final verse and chorus bring the story to a close.

COAT OF MANY COLORS

Words and Music by
DOLLY PARTON

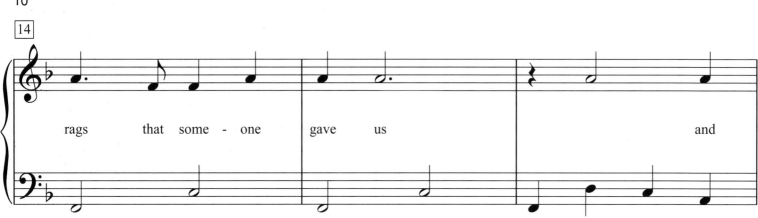

rags   that some - one   gave   us   and

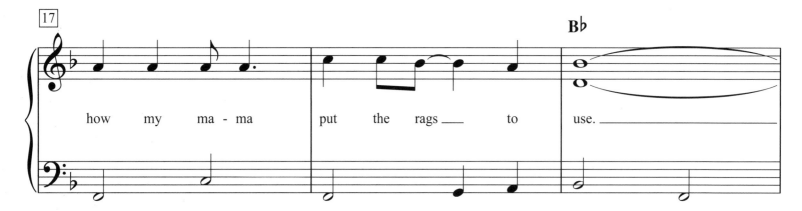

how   my   ma - ma   put   the   rags ___ to   use. ___

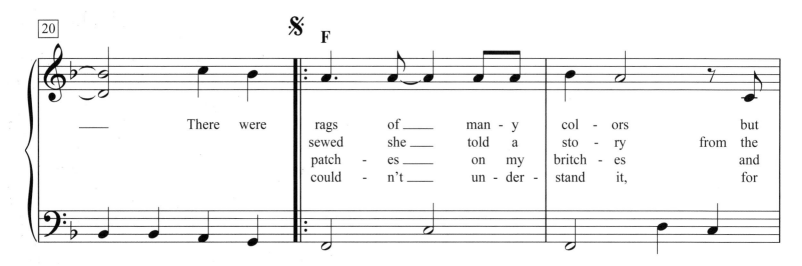

There   were   rags   of ___ man - y   col - ors   but
                 sewed   she ___ told   a   sto - ry   from   the
                 patch - es ___ on   my   britch - es   and
                 could - n't ___ un - der - stand   it,   for

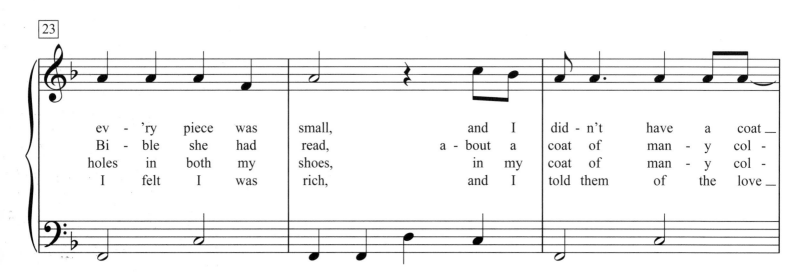

ev - 'ry   piece   was   small,   and   I   did - n't   have   a   coat ___
Bi - ble   she   had   read,   a - bout   a   coat   of   man - y   col -
holes   in   both   my   shoes,   in   my   coat   of   man - y   col -
I   felt   I   was   rich,   and   I   told   them   of   the   love ___

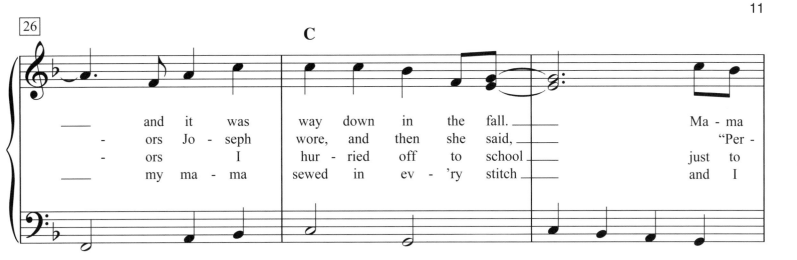

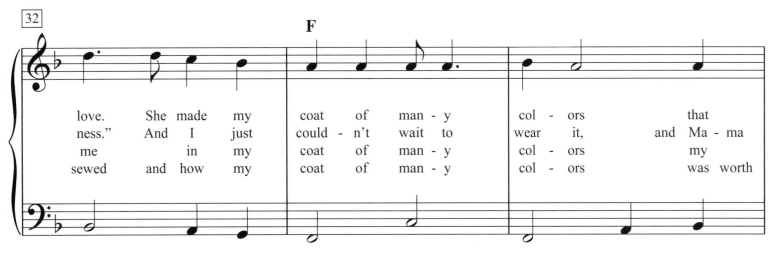

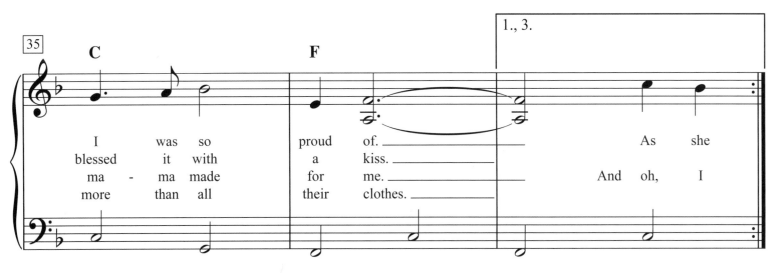

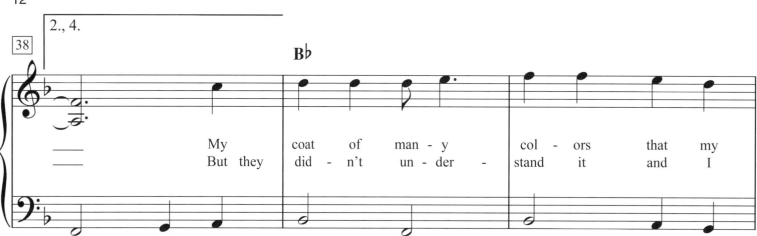

My coat of man - y col - ors that my
But they did - n't un - der - stand it and I

ma - ma made for me
tried to make them see that

made on - ly from
one is on - ly

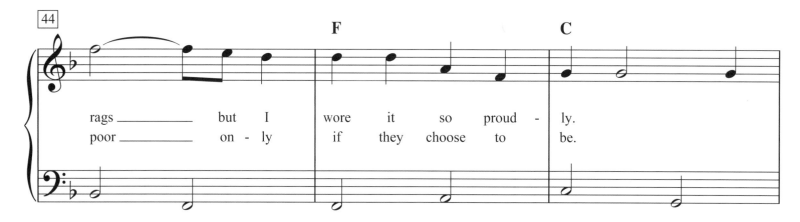

rags _____ but I wore it so proud - ly.
poor _____ on - ly if they choose to be.

Al - though we had no mon - ey. I was
Now I know we had no mon - ey, but I was

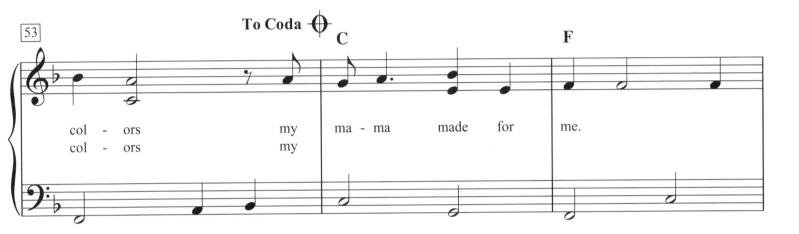

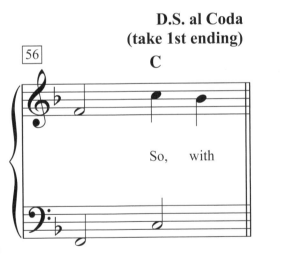

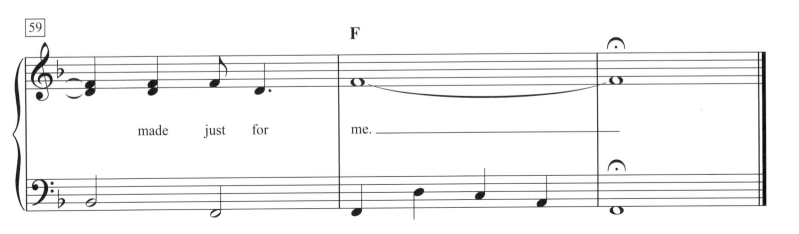

ACHY BREAKY HEART
(Don't Tell My Heart)

Words and Music by
DON VON TRESS

Steady beat

You can tell the world you nev - er was my girl. _____
You can tell your ma I moved to Ar - kan - sas. _____

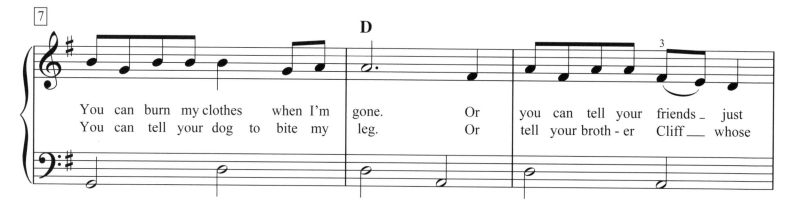

You can burn my clothes when I'm gone. Or you can tell your friends _ just
You can tell your dog to bite my leg. Or tell your broth - er Cliff _ whose

what a fool I've been and laugh and joke a - bout me on the
fist can tell my lip, he nev - er real - ly liked me an - y -

phone. ___ Or, You can tell my arms go back ___ to the farm.
way. ___ tell your Aunt Lou - ise, tell an - y - thing you please. My -

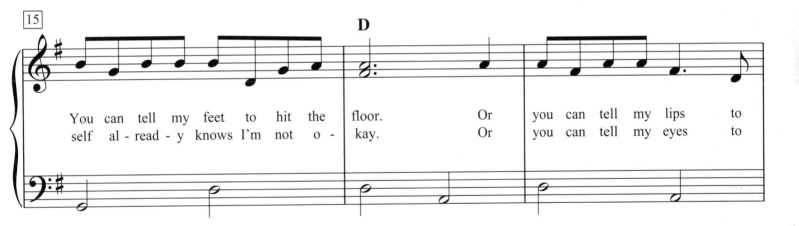

You can tell my feet to hit the floor. Or you can tell my lips to
self al - read - y knows I'm not o - kay. Or you can tell my eyes to

tell my fin - ger - tips they won't be reach - ing out for you no more. ___
watch out for my mind. It might be walk - ing out on me to - day. ___ But

(D.S.) Don't tell my heart, }
don't tell my heart, } my ach - y break - y heart, __ I just don't think he'd un - der -

stand. And if you tell my heart, my ach - y break - y heart, __ he

might blow __ up and kill this man. Oh.

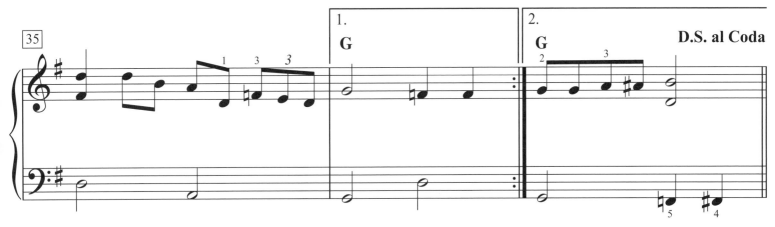

man. Don't tell my heart, my ach - y break - y heart, I

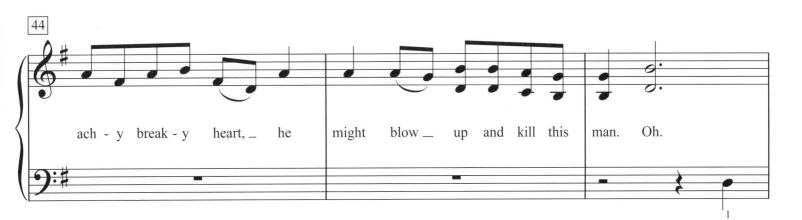

just don't think he'd un - der - stand. And if you tell my heart, my

ach - y break - y heart, he might blow up and kill this man. Oh.

CRAZY

Words and Music by
WILLIE NELSON

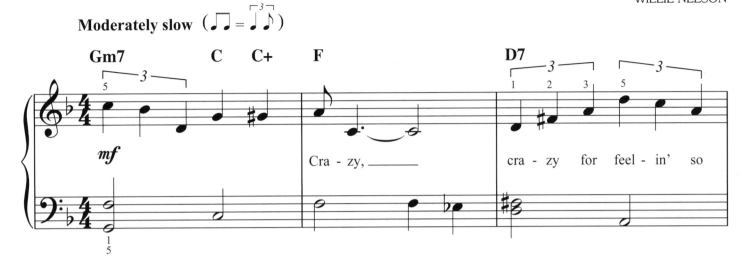

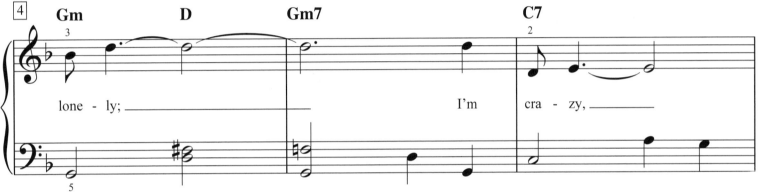

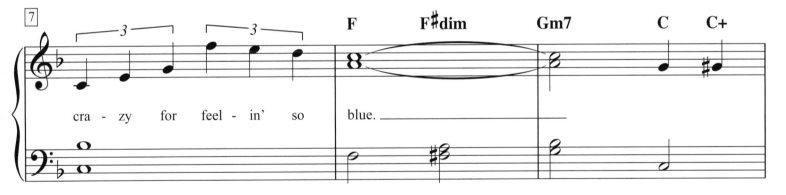

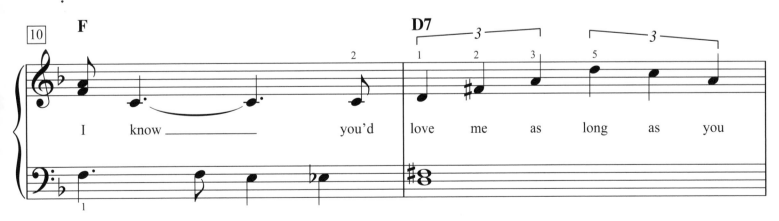

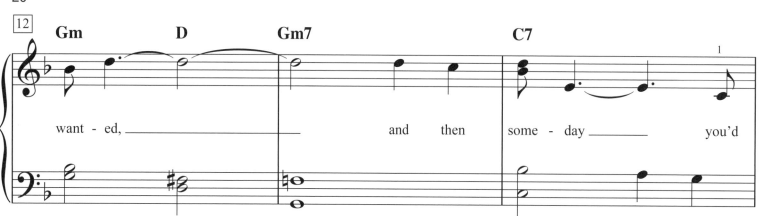

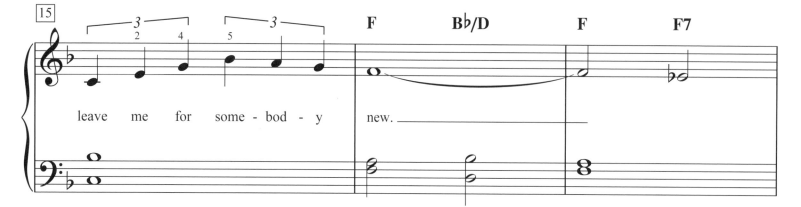

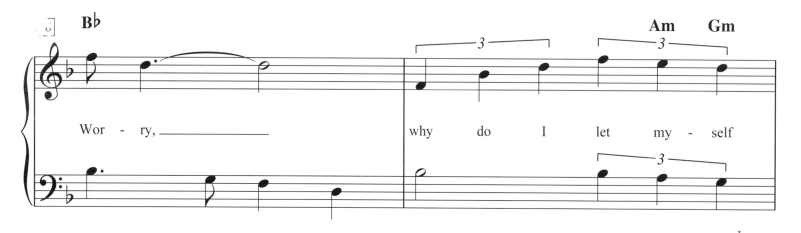

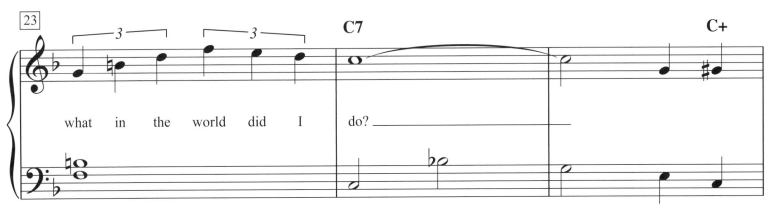

what in the world did I do? _____

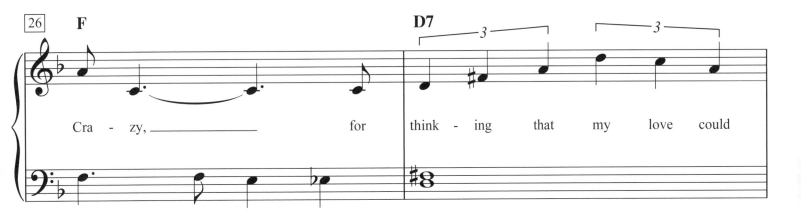

Cra - zy, _____ for think - ing that my love could

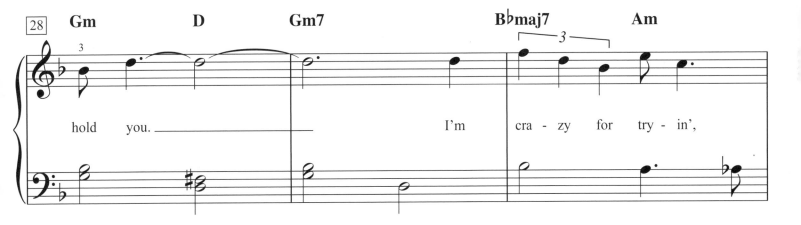

hold you. _____ I'm cra - zy for try - in',

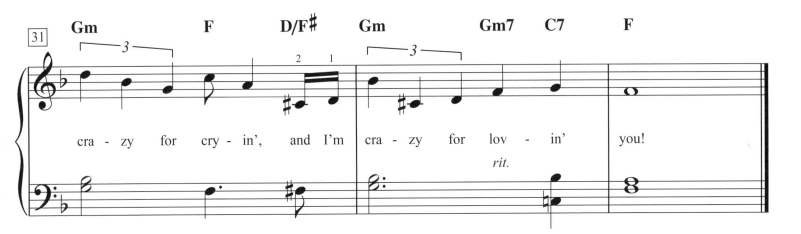

cra - zy for cry - in', and I'm cra - zy for lov - in' you!

rit.

AMAZED

Words and Music by MARV GREEN,
CHRIS LINDSEY and AIMEE MAYO

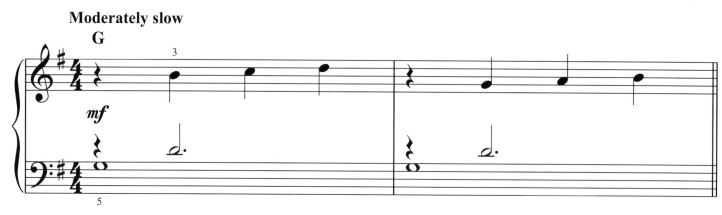

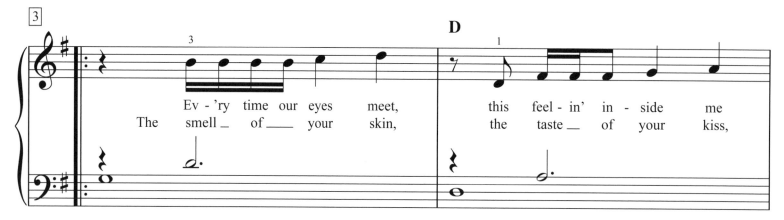

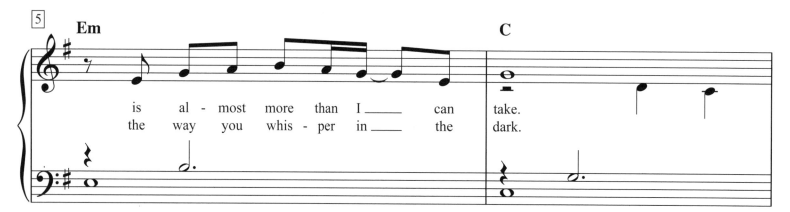

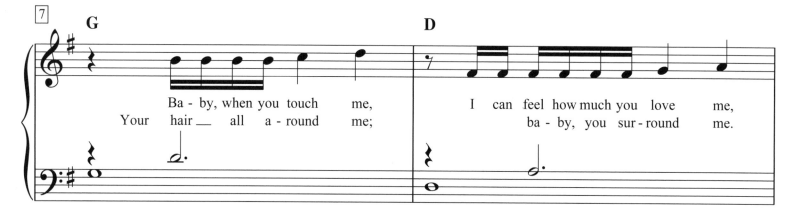

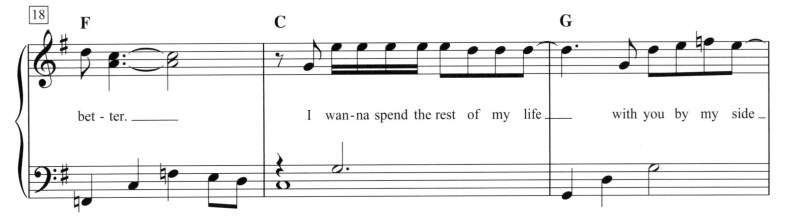

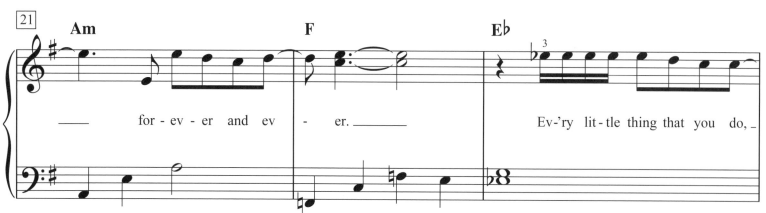

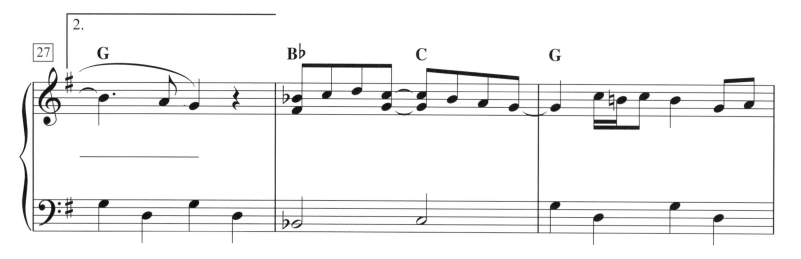

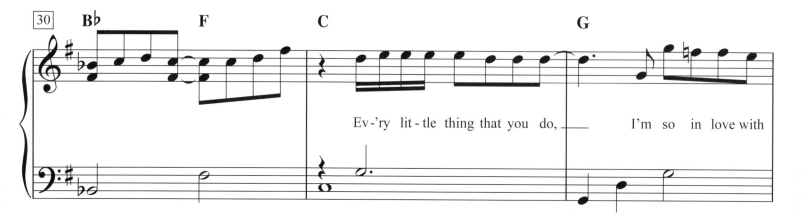

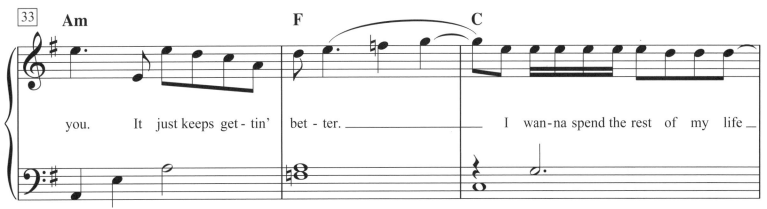

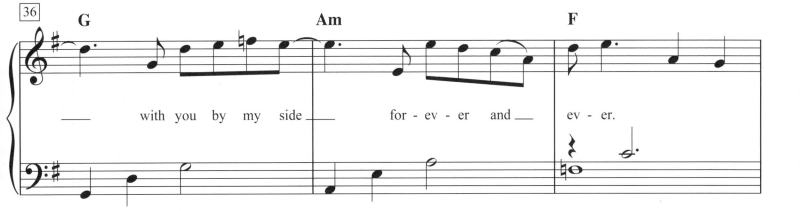

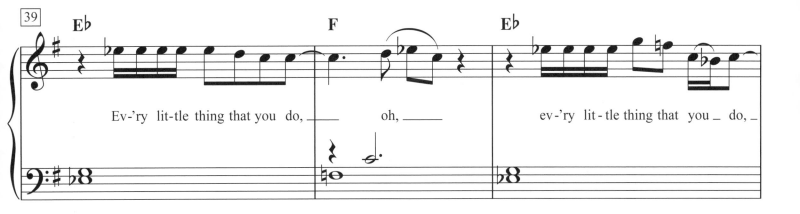

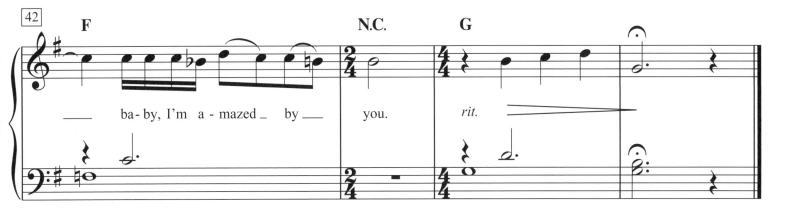

BE A LIGHT

Words and Music by THOMAS RHETT,
JOSH MILLER, JOSH THOMPSON
and MATTHEW DRAGSTREM

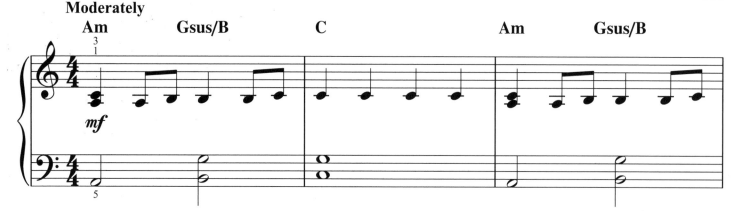

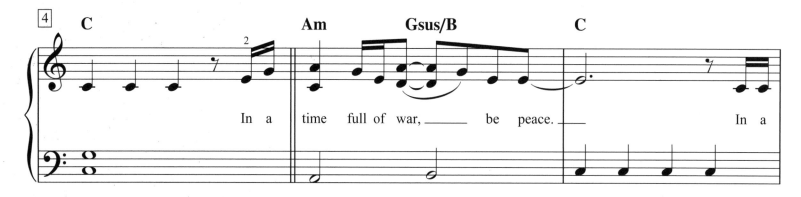

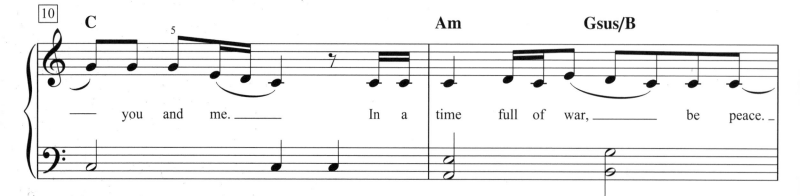

In a world full of hate, _____ be a light. _____

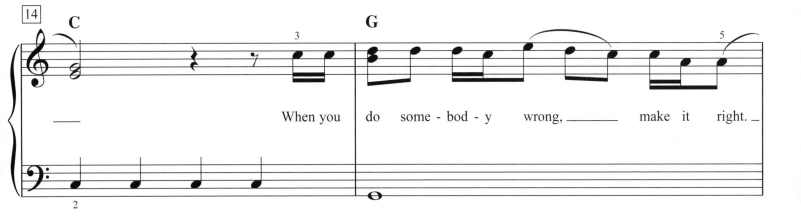

When you do some-bod-y wrong, _____ make it right. _____

_____ Don't _ hide in the dark; _ you were born to shine. _ In a

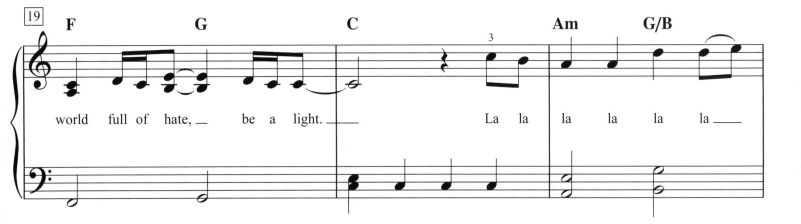

world full of hate, _ be a light. _____ La la la la la la _____

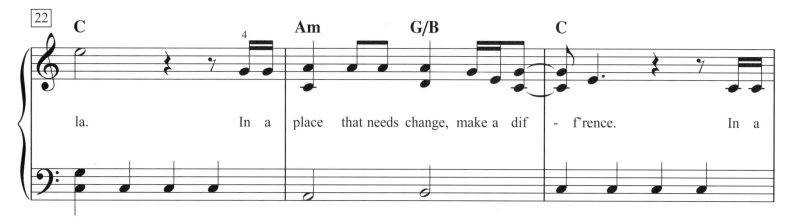

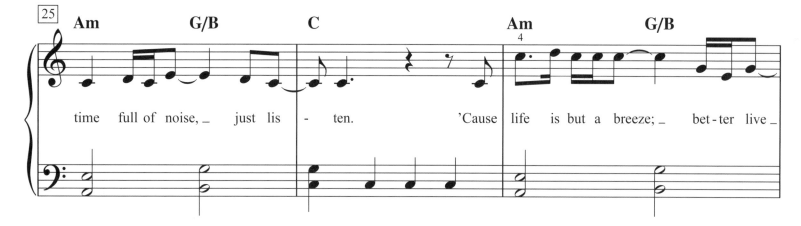

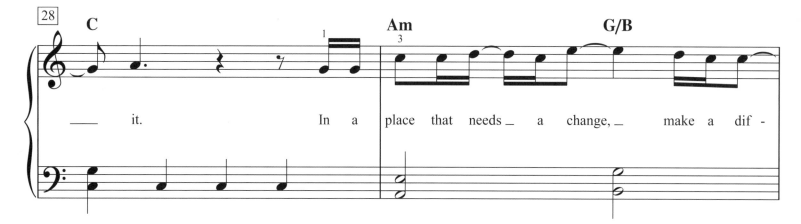

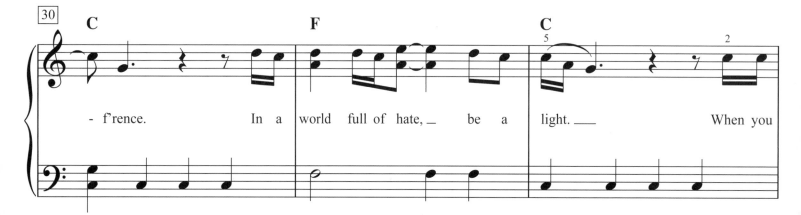

do some-bod-y wrong, __ make it right. __ Oh, don't hide in the dark; __ you were

born to shine. __ In a world full of hate, __ be a light. __

__ La la la la la la __ la. La la

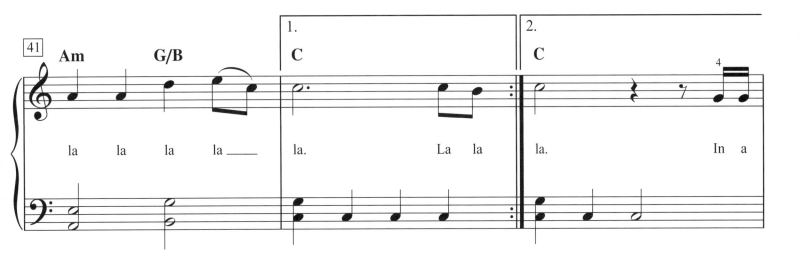

la la la la __ la. La la la. In a

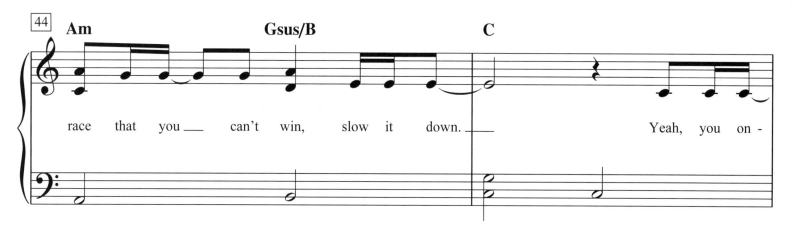

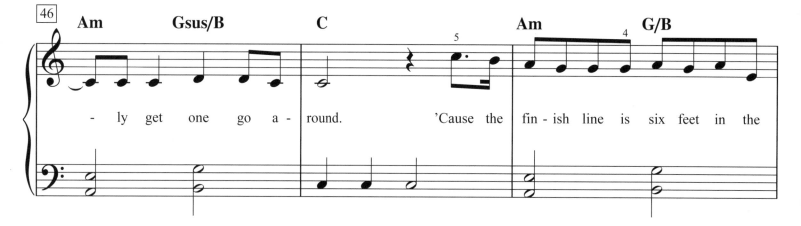

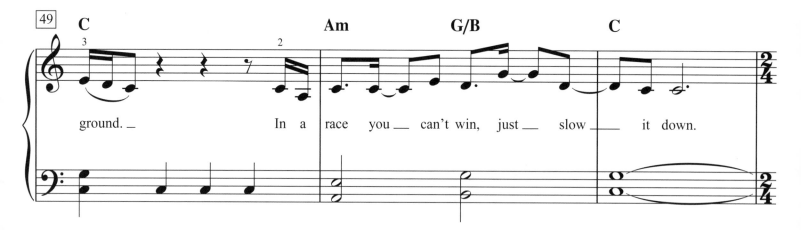

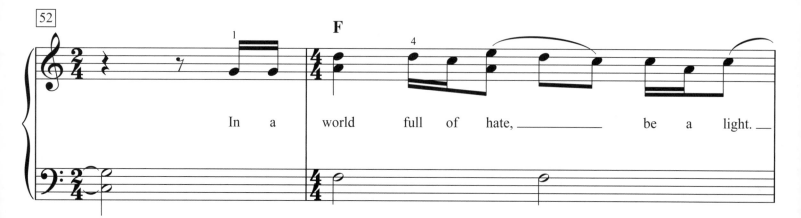

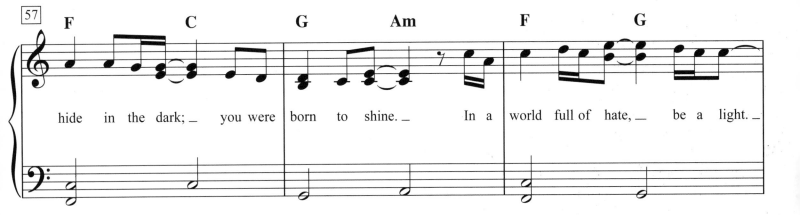

BLESS THE BROKEN ROAD

Words and Music by MARCUS HUMMON,
BOBBY BOYD and JEFF HANNA

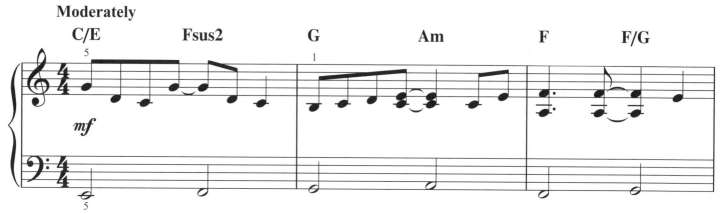

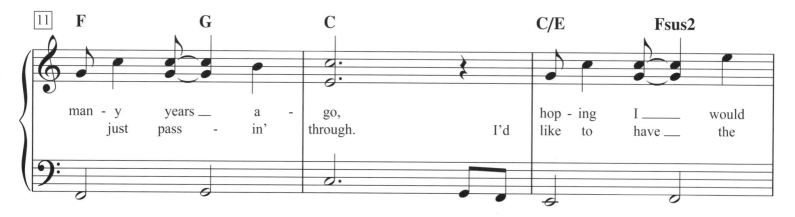

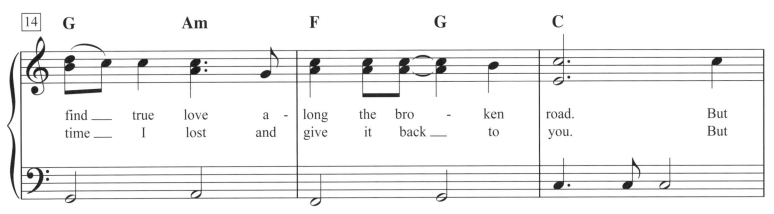

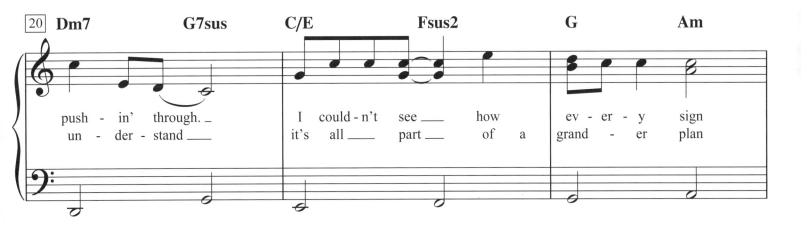

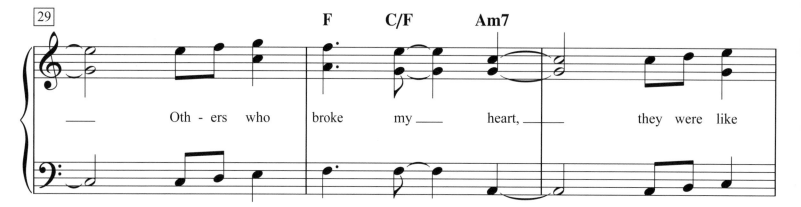

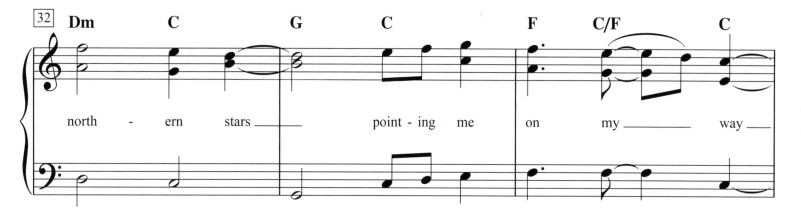

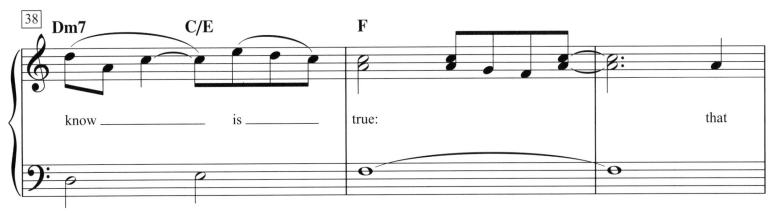

know _____ is _____ true: that

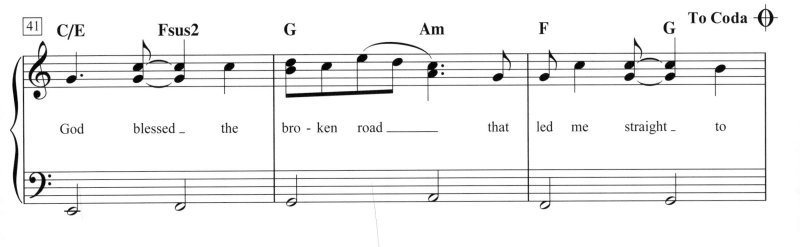

God   blessed _ the   bro - ken   road _____   that led me   straight _ to

you.

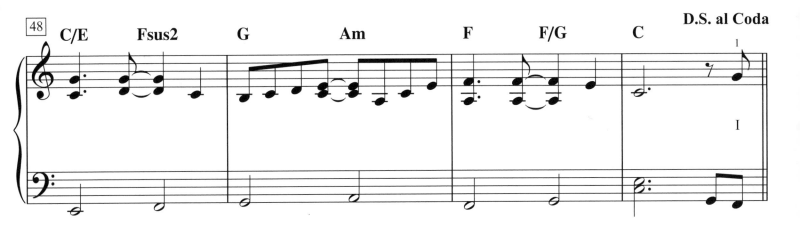

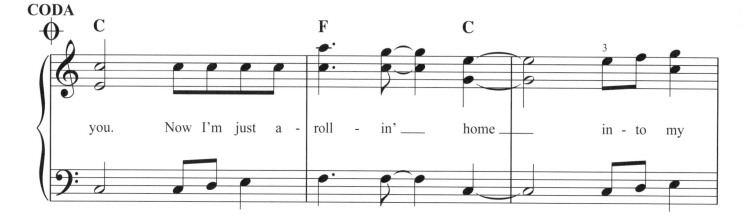

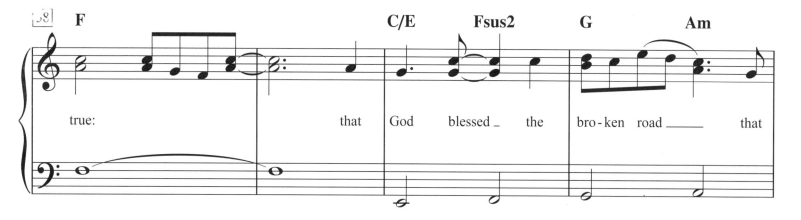

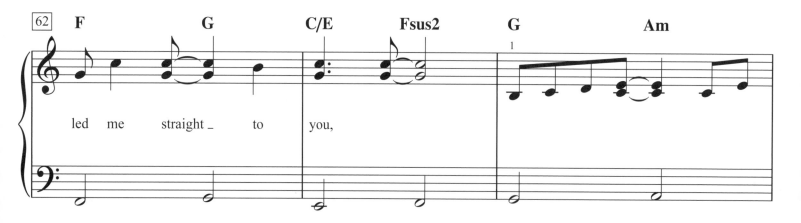

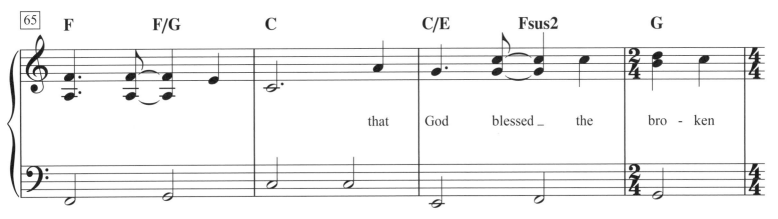

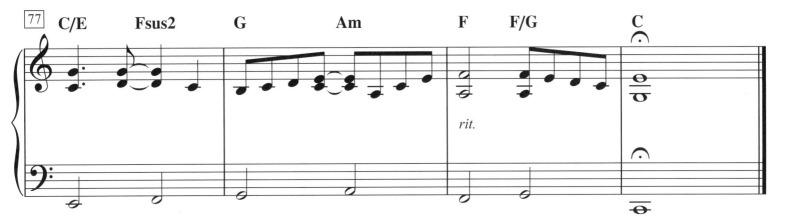

THE DEVIL WENT DOWN TO GEORGIA

Words and Music by CHARLIE DANIELS,
JOHN THOMAS CRAIN, JR., WILLIAM JOEL DiGREGORIO,
FRED LAROY EDWARDS, CHARLES FRED HAYWARD
and JAMES WAINWRIGHT MARSHALL

Fast Hoedown

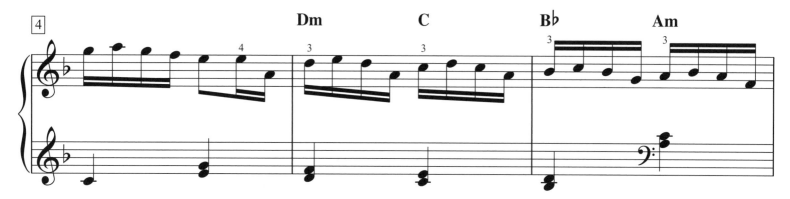

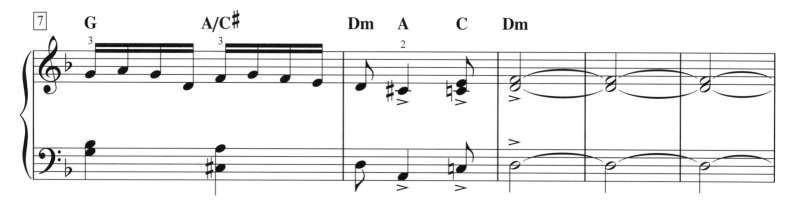

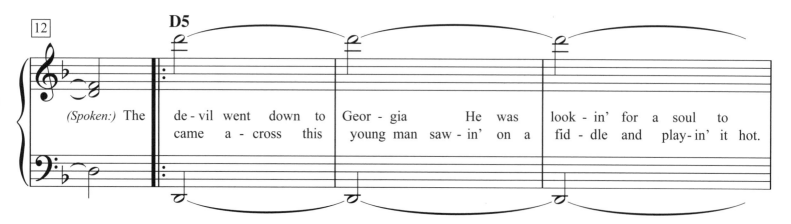

(Spoken:) The de-vil went down to Geor-gia He was look-in' for a soul to
came a-cross this young man saw-in' on a fid-dle and play-in' it hot.

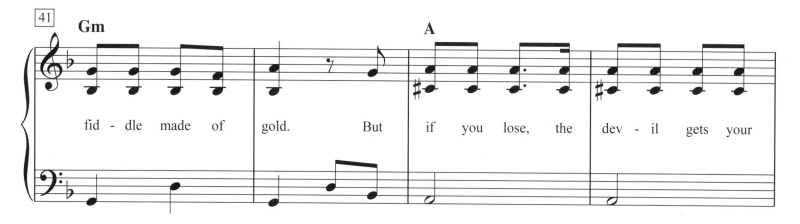

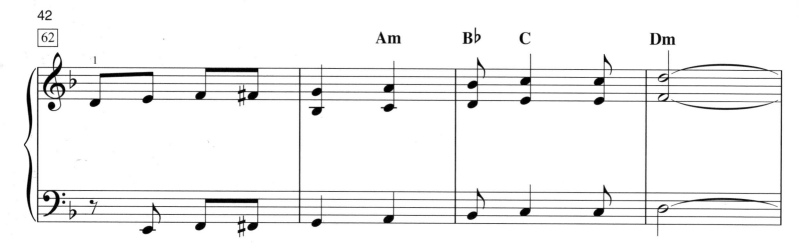

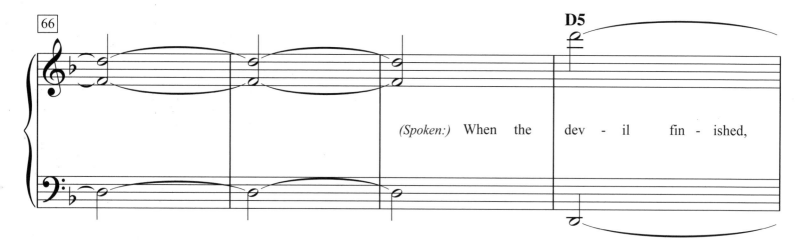

(Spoken:) When the dev - il fin - ished,

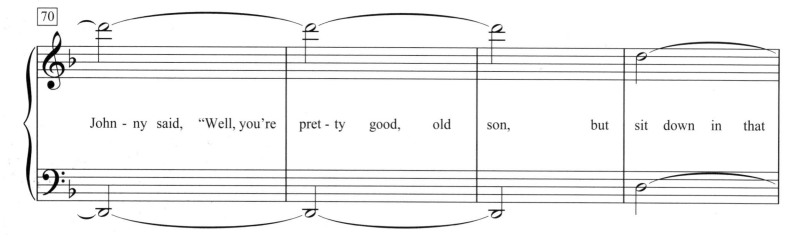

John - ny said, "Well, you're pret - ty good, old son, but sit down in that

chair right there and let me show you how it's done."

(Sung:) Fire on the moun - tain.

Run, boys, run. The dev-il's in the House of the

Ris - ing Sun. Chick-en in the bread-pan

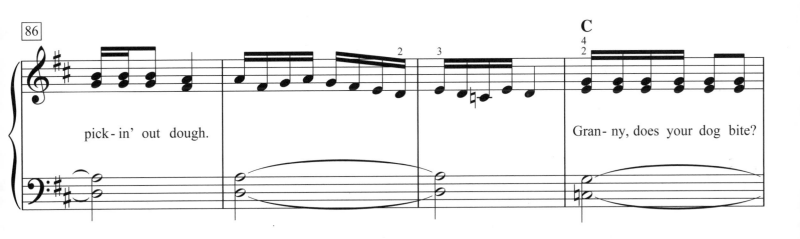

pick-in' out dough. Gran-ny, does your dog bite?

No, child, no.

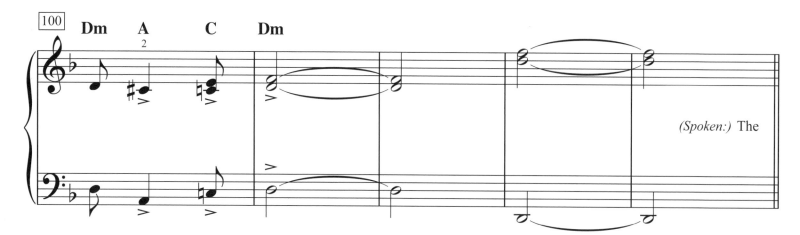

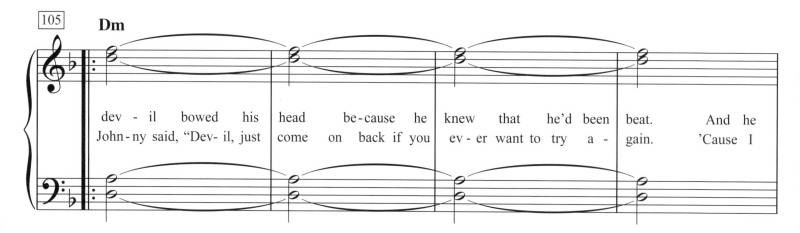

dev - il bowed his head be - cause he knew that he'd been beat. And he
John - ny said, "Dev - il, just come on back if you ev - er want to try a - gain. 'Cause I

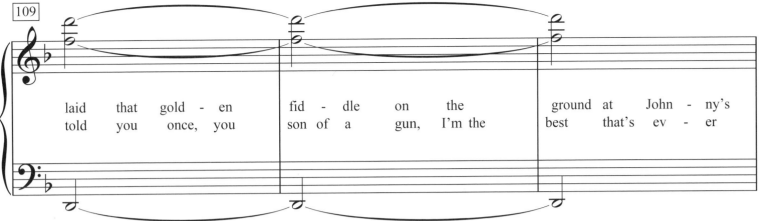

laid   that   gold - en   fid - dle   on   the   ground at   John - ny's
told   you   once,   you   son of a   gun, I'm the   best   that's ev - er

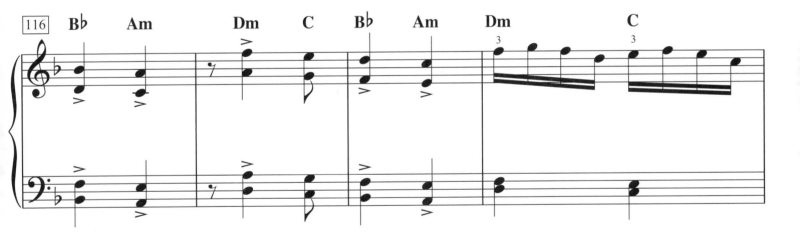

feet.
been.

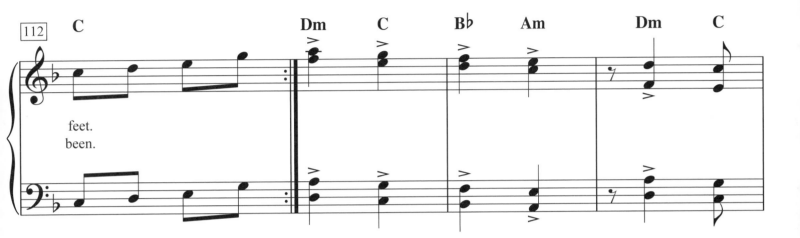

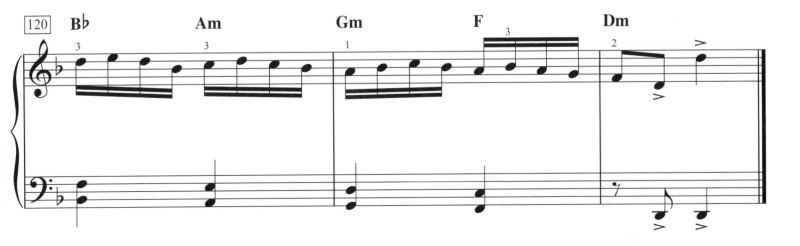

FOREVER AND EVER, AMEN

Words and Music by PAUL OVERSTREET
and DON SCHLITZ

Moderately fast

You may think that I'm _____ talk - in' fool - ish,
you're not just time _____ that I'm kill - in'.

you've heard that I'm wild _____ and I'm free. _____
I'm no long - er one _____ of those guys. _____

You may won - der how _____ I can prom - ise you now _____
As sure as I live _____ this love that I give _____

_____ this love that I feel _____ for you al -
_____ is gon - na be yours _____ un - til the

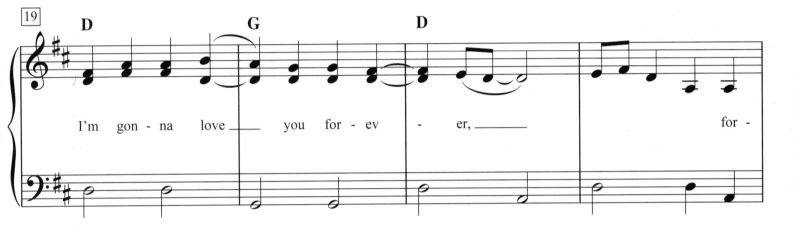

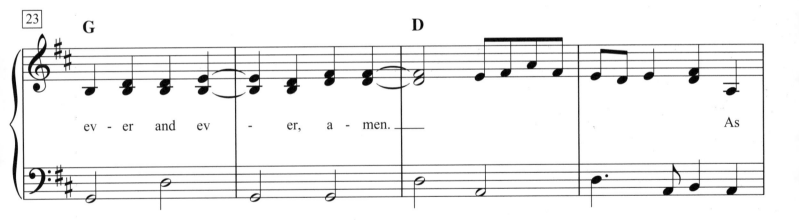

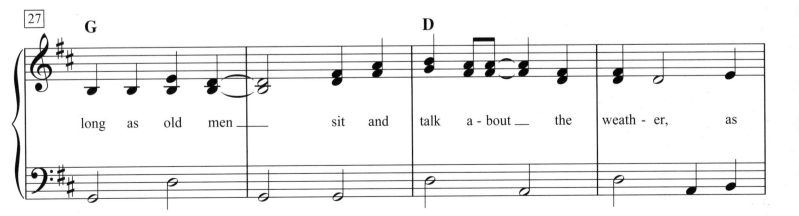

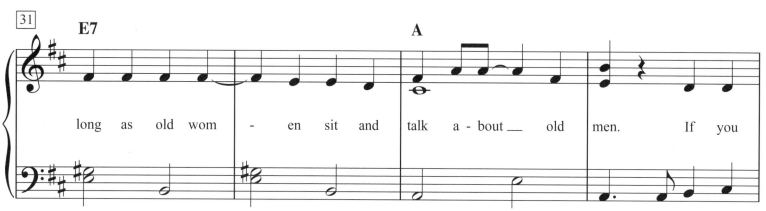

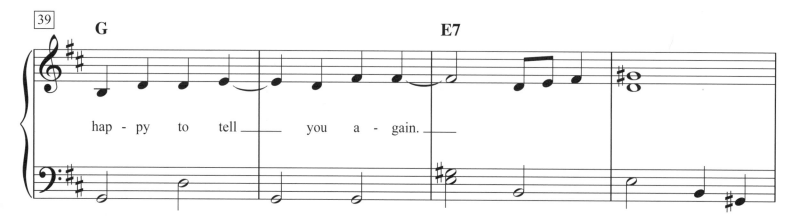

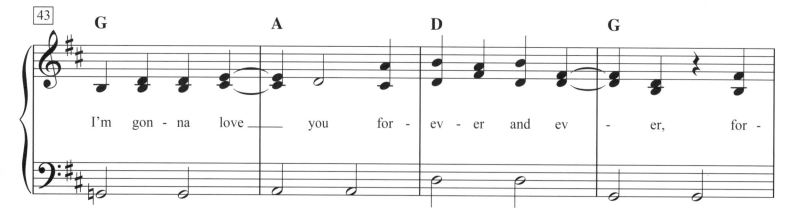

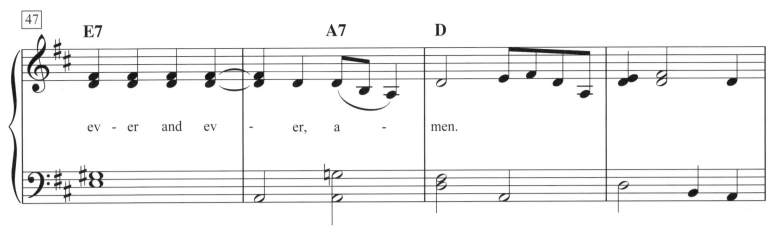

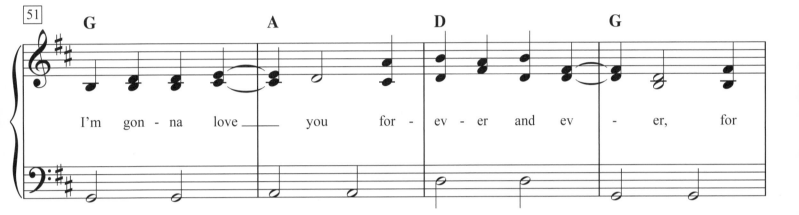

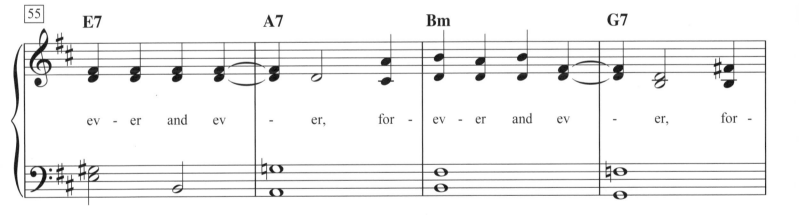

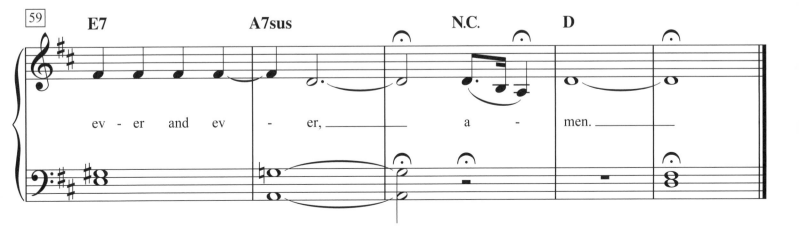

THE GAMBLER

Words and Music by
DON SCHLITZ

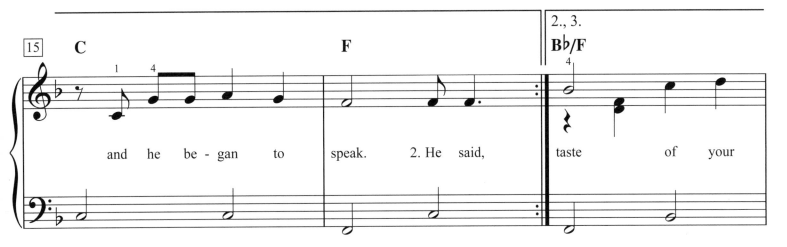

and he be-gan to speak. 2. He said, taste of your

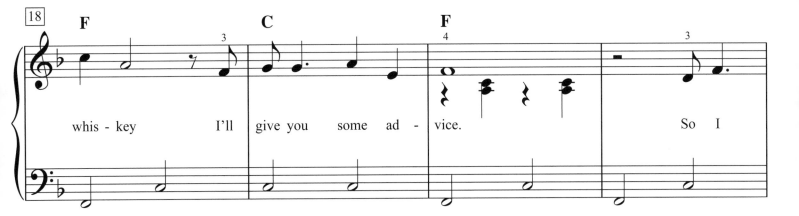

whis-key I'll give you some ad - vice. So I

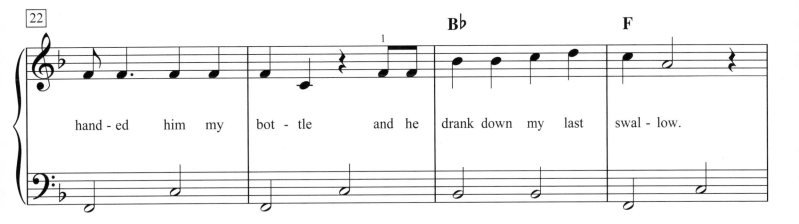

hand - ed him my bot - tle and he drank down my last swal - low.

Then he bummed a cig - a - rette __ and asked me for a light. And the

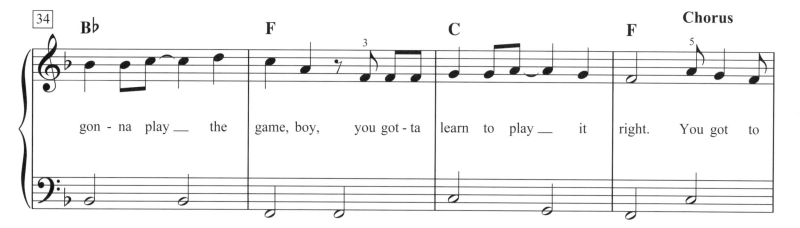

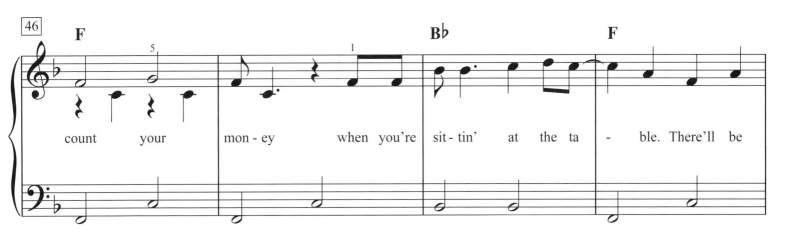

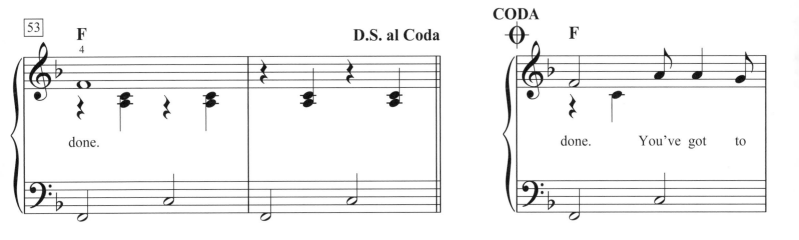

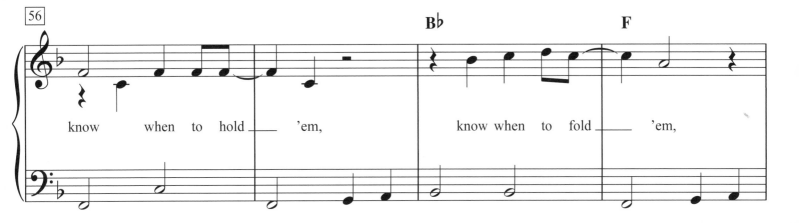

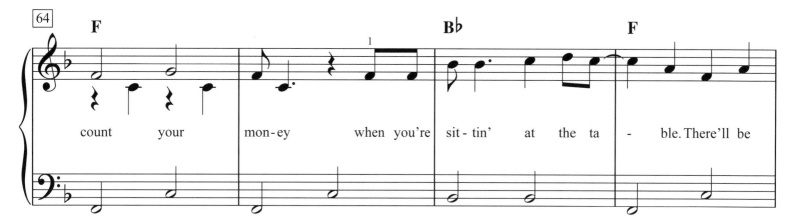

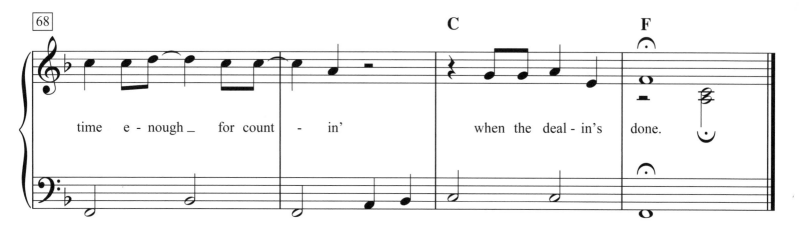

Additional Lyrics

3. Ev'ry gambler knows that the secret to survivin'
   Is knowin' what to throw away and knowin' what to keep.
   'Cause ev'ry hand's a winner and ev'ry hand's a loser
   And the best that you can hope for is to die in your sleep.
   And when he'd finished speakin', he turned back towards the window
   Crushed out his cigarette and faded off to sleep.
   And somewhere in the darkness, the gambler, he broke even
   But in his final words I found an ace that I could keep.
   Chorus

GREEN GREEN GRASS OF HOME

Words and Music by
CURLY PUTMAN

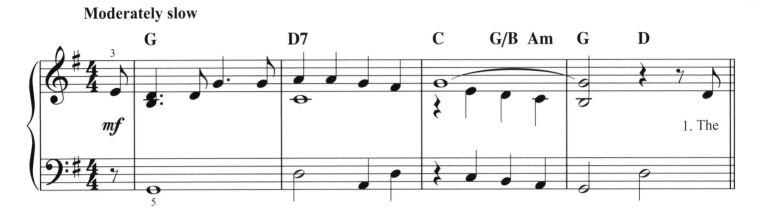

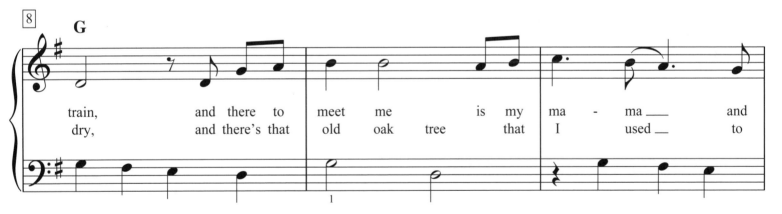

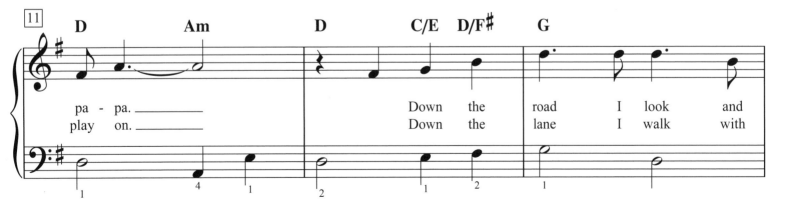

56

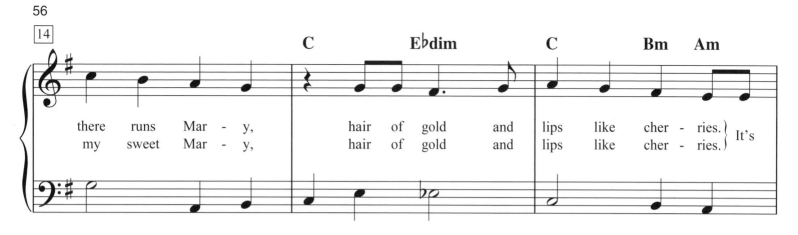

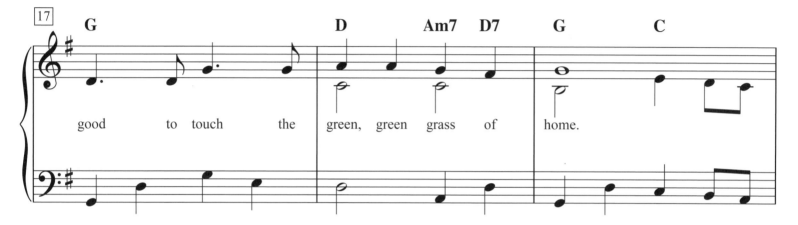

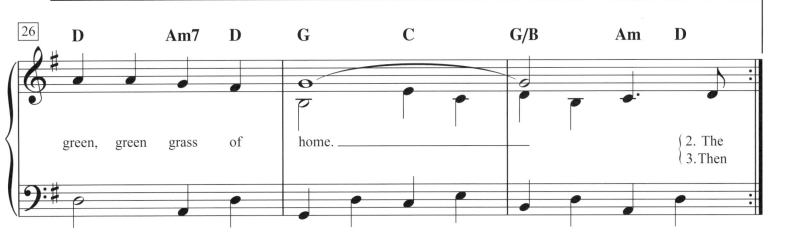

green, green grass of home. 2. The 3. Then

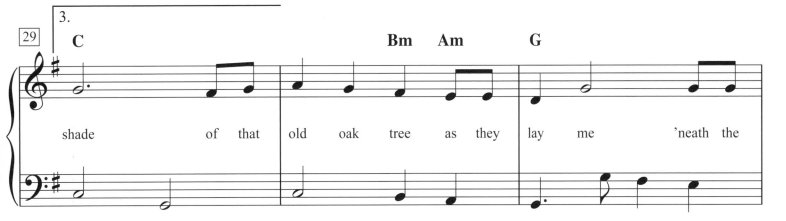

shade of that old oak tree as they lay me 'neath the

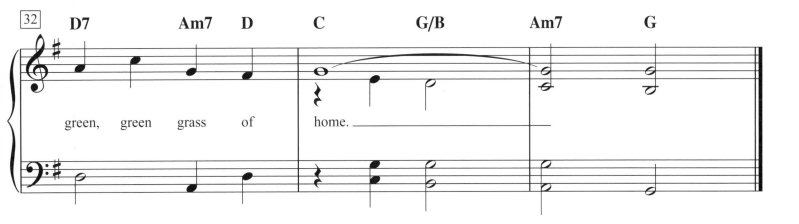

green, green grass of home.

Additional Lyrics

3. Then I awake and look around me
   At four gray walls that surround me,
   And I realize that I was only dreaming.
   For there's a guard and there's a sad old padre,
   Arm in arm we'll walk at daybreak,
   Again I'll touch the green, green grass of home.

   Yes, they'll all come to see me
   In the shade of that old oak tree
   As they lay me 'neath the green, green grass of home.

GOD BLESS THE U.S.A.

Words and Music by
LEE GREENWOOD

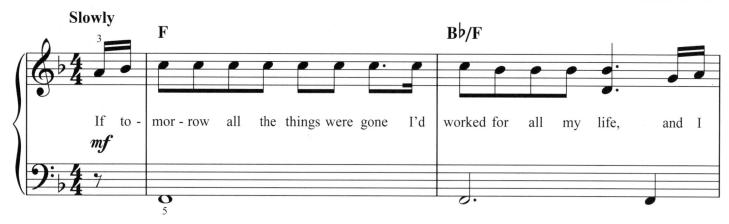

If to-mor-row all the things were gone I'd worked for all my life, and I

had to start a-gain ___ with just my chil-dren and my wife, I'd

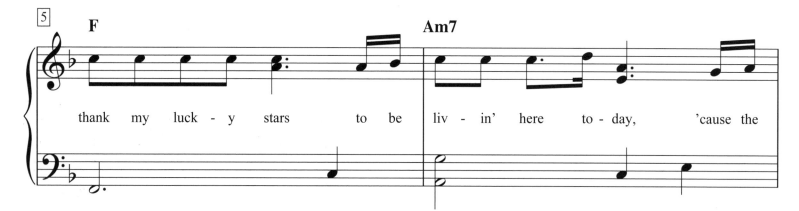

thank my luck-y stars to be liv-in' here to-day, 'cause the

flag still stands for free-dom, and they can't take that a-way! ___

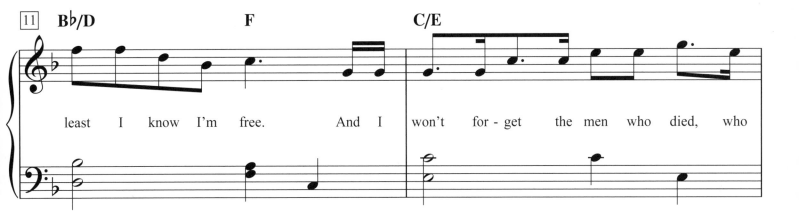

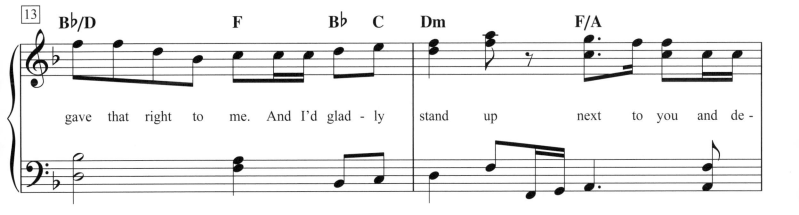

God bless the U. S. A.

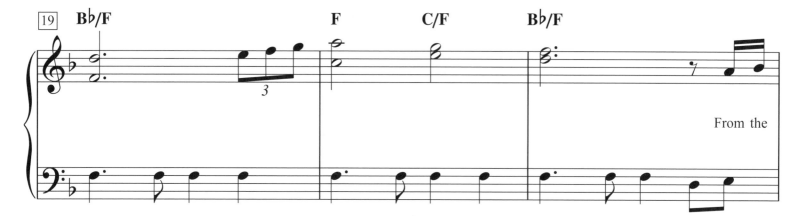

From the

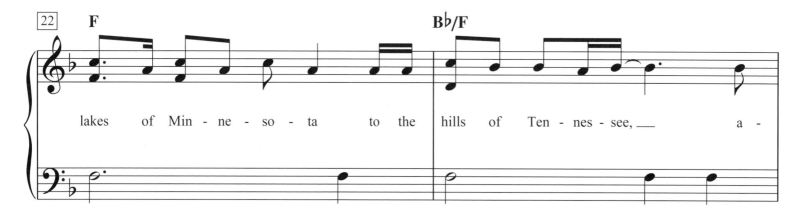

lakes of Min - ne - so - ta to the hills of Ten - nes - see, __ a -

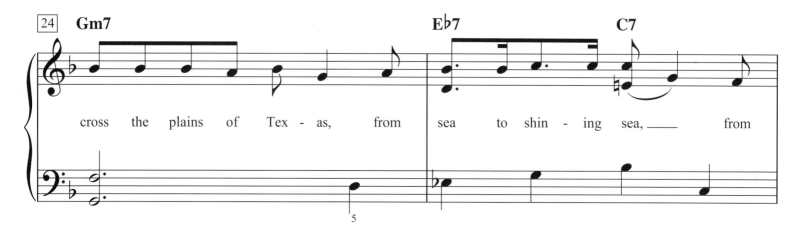

cross the plains of Tex - as, from sea to shin - ing sea, __ from

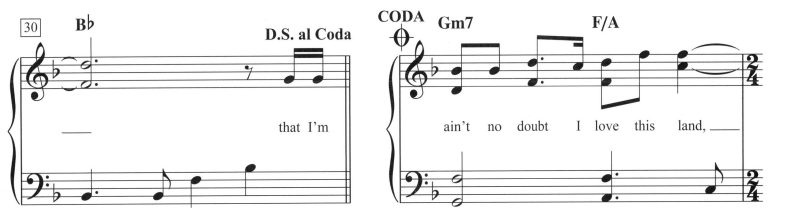

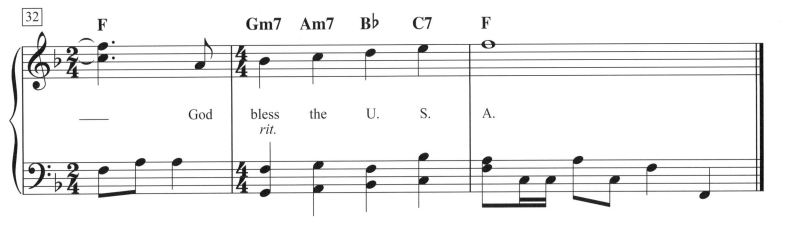

GRANDPA
(Tell Me 'Bout the Good Old Days)

Words and Music by
JAMIE O'HARA

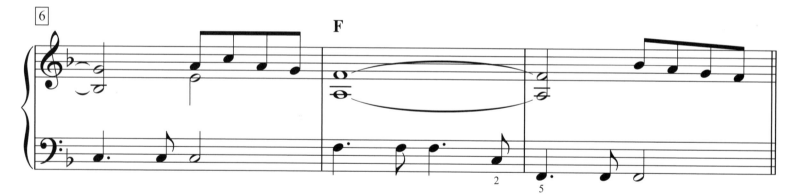

Grand - pa, _____
Grand - pa, _____

tell me 'bout the   good old   days. __
ev - 'ry - thing is   chang - in'   fast. __

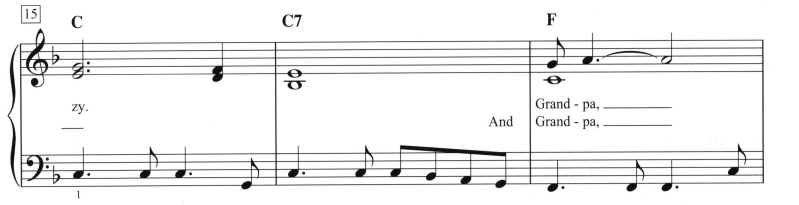

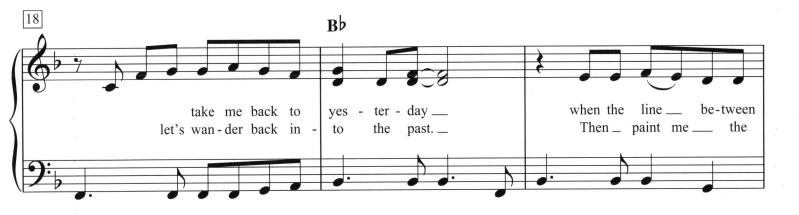

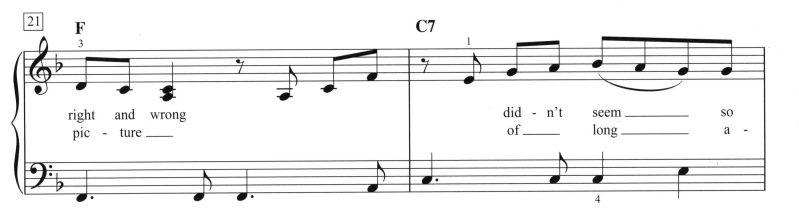

23 F ... Bᵇ ... 2

ha - zy.⟩
go. ___⟩

Did lov - ers real - ly fall in love to

26

stay, and stand be - side each oth - er come what may? Was a prom - ise real - ly

29 C7 ... F

some - thing peo - ple ___ kept, not just some-thing they would say? ___

32 Bᵇ

Did fam - 'lies real - ly bow their heads to pray? Did dad - dies real - ly

never go a - way? Oh, _____ oh, _____ Grand - pa, _____

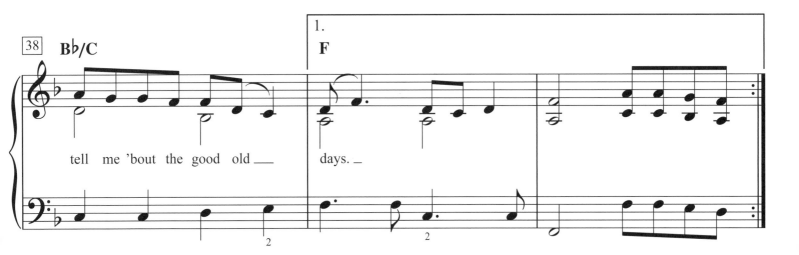

tell me 'bout the good old _____ days. _____

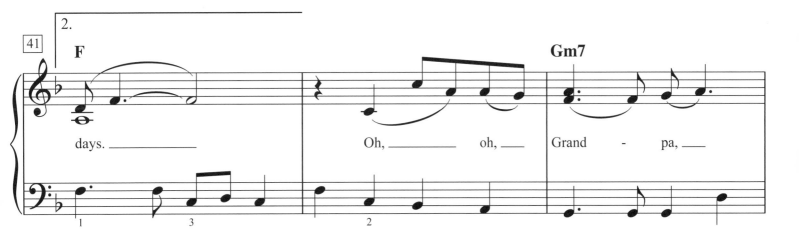

days. _____ Oh, _____ oh, _____ Grand - pa, _____

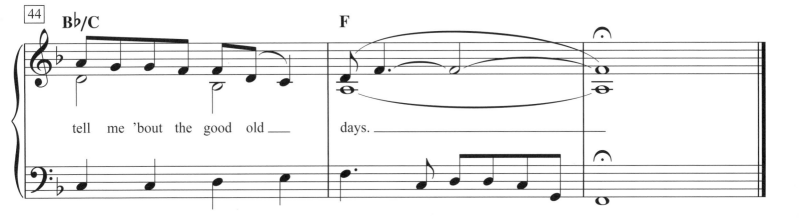

tell me 'bout the good old _____ days. _____

LOVE ME TENDER

Words and Music by ELVIS PRESLEY
and VERA MATSON

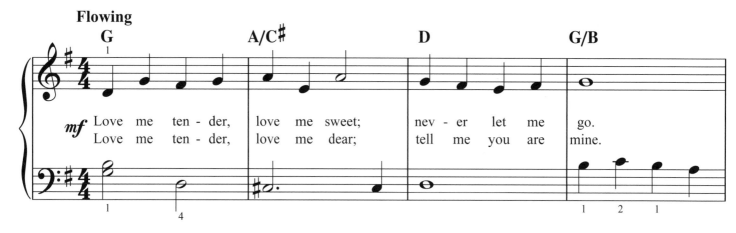

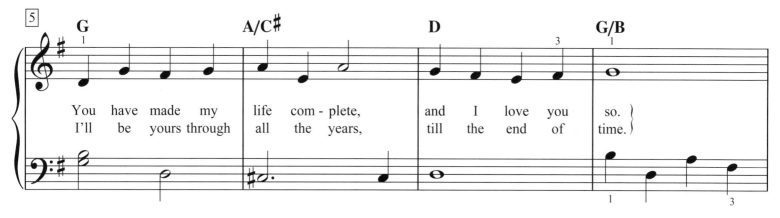

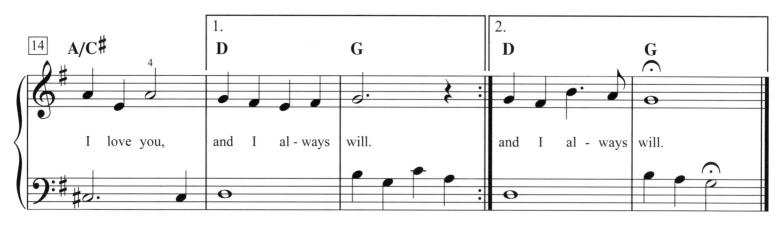

THE HOUSE THAT BUILT ME

Words and Music by TOM DOUGLAS
and ALLEN SHAMBLIN

Moderately fast, in 2

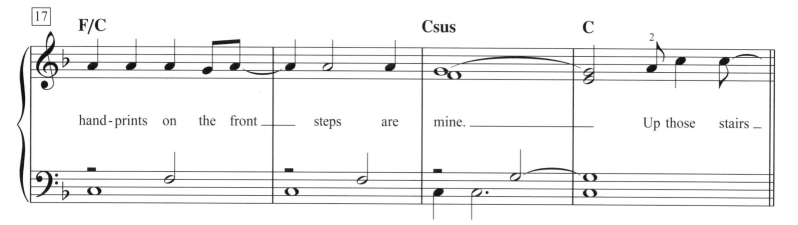

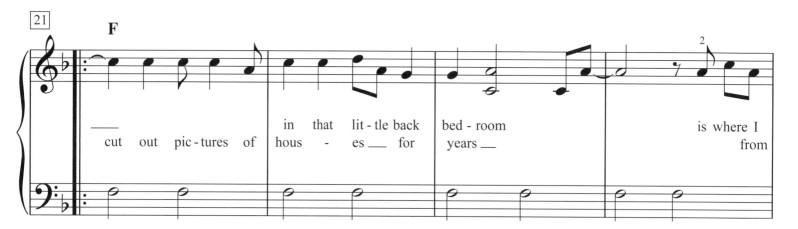

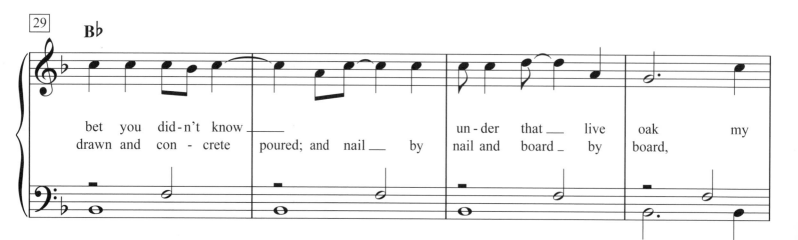

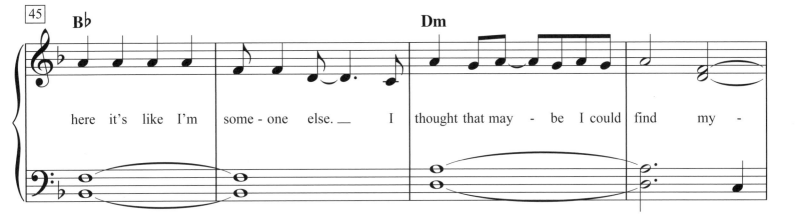

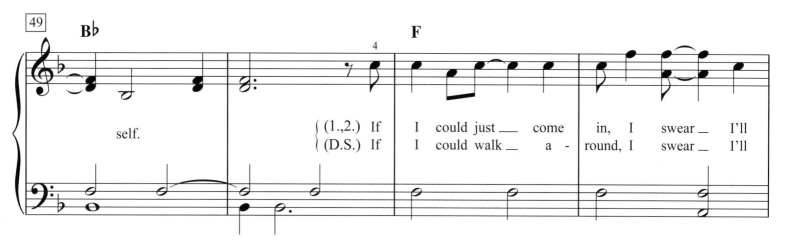

self.

(1.,2.) If I could just ___ come in, I swear ___ I'll

(D.S.) If I could walk ___ a - round, I swear ___ I'll

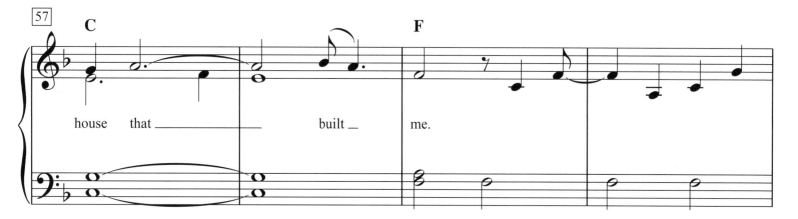

leave.)

leave.)

Won't take noth - in' but a mem-o - ry _____ from the

To Coda

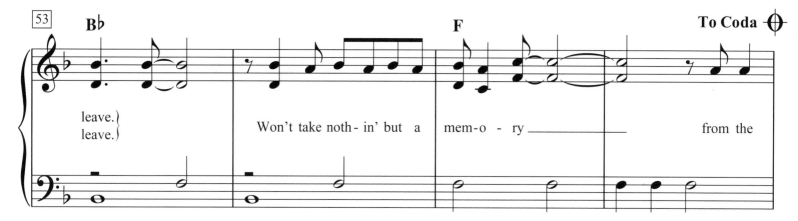

house that _____ built ___ me.

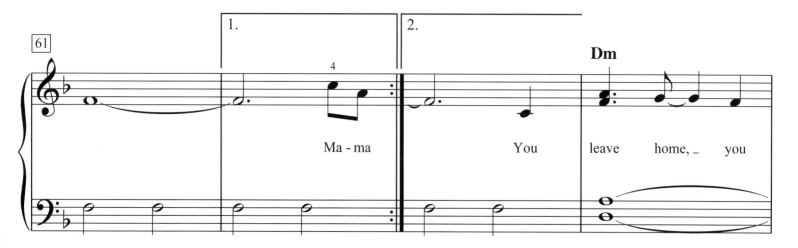

1.

Ma - ma

2.

You leave home, ___ you

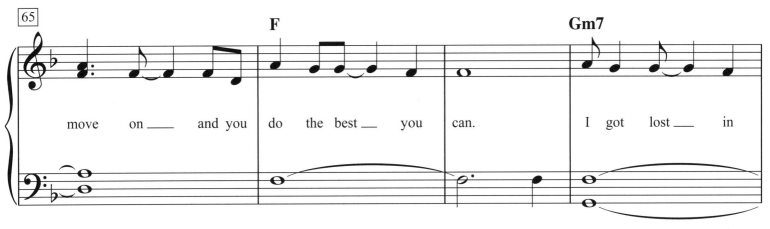

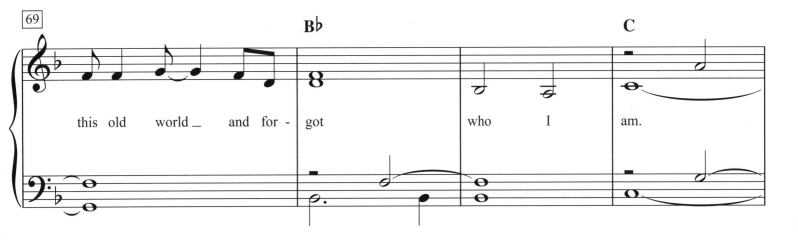

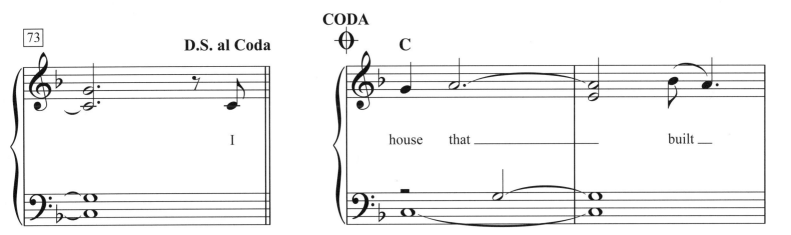

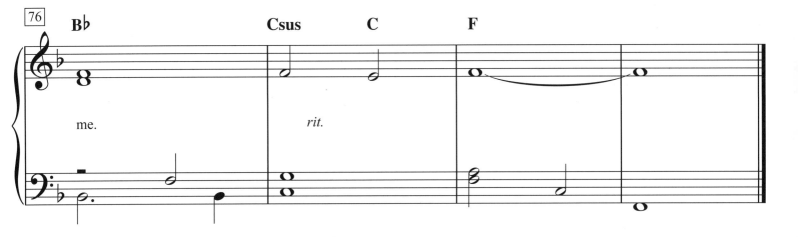

I HOPE YOU DANCE

Words and Music by TIA SILLERS
and MARK D. SANDERS

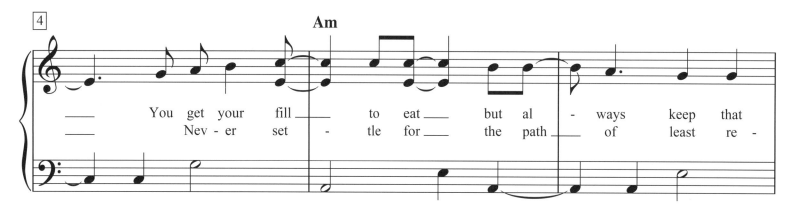

hope you nev - er lose _____ your sense of won - der. _____
nev - er fear _____ those _____ moun - tains in the dis - tance. _____

_____ You get your fill _____ to eat _____ but al - ways keep that
_____ Nev - er set - tle for _____ the path _____ of least re -

hun - ger. _____ May you nev - er take _____ one
sist - ance. _____ Liv - in' might mean tak - in'

sin - gle breath _____ for grant - ed. _____ God for - bid _____
chanc - es if they're worth tak - in'. _____ Lov - in' might _____

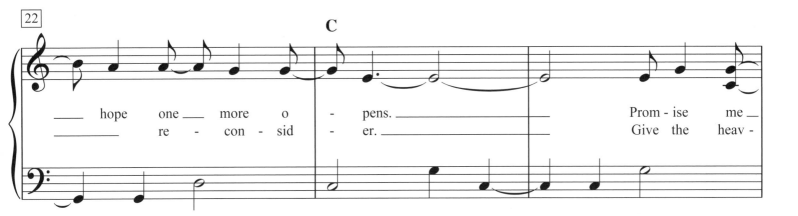

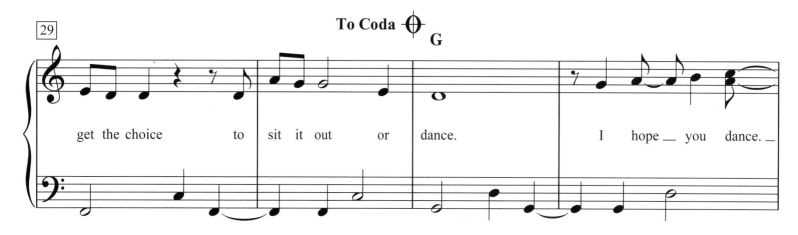

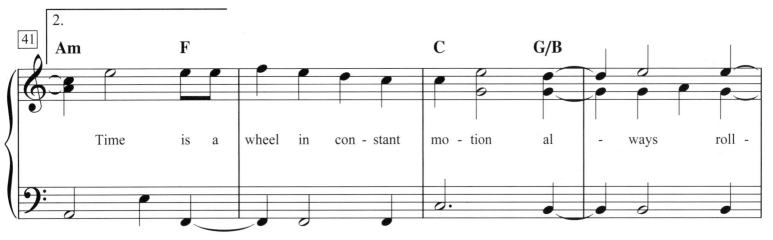

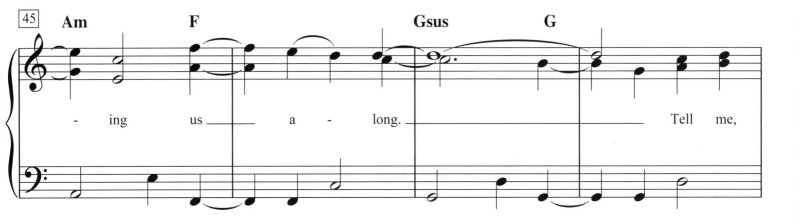

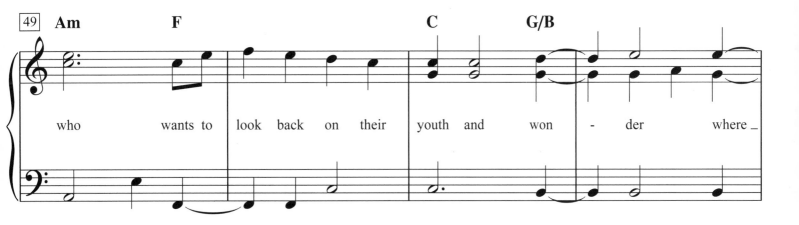

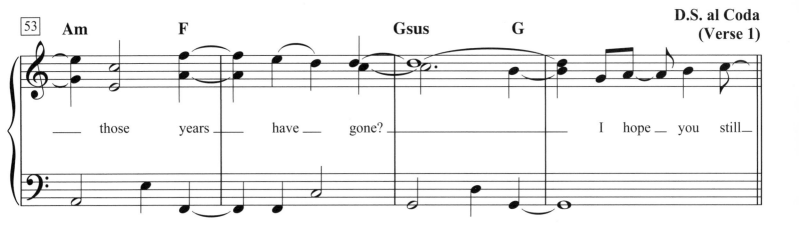

CODA

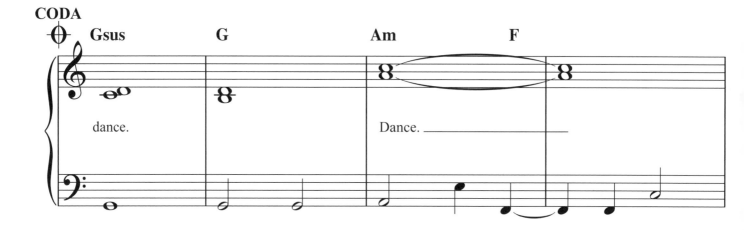

dance.

Dance. _____

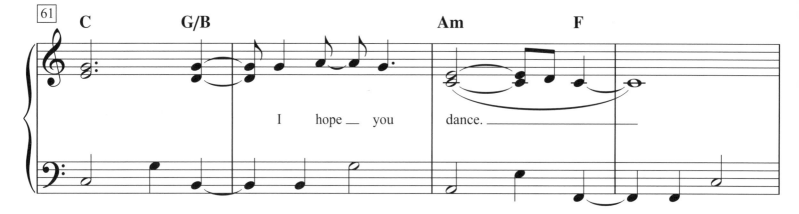

I hope __ you dance. _____

I hope __ you dance. __ Time is a

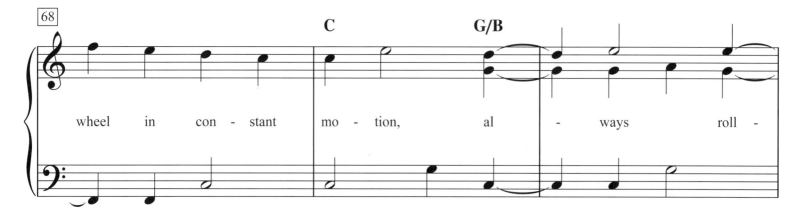

wheel in con - stant mo - tion, al - ways roll -

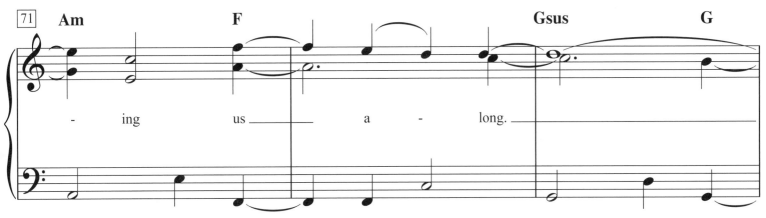

-ing us ____ a - long. ____

____ Tell me, who wants to look back on their

youth and won - der where ____ those years ____

____ have ____ gone? ____

MAY THE BIRD OF PARADISE FLY UP YOUR NOSE

Words and Music by
NEAL MERRITT

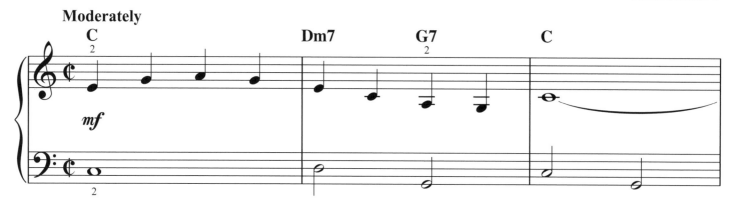

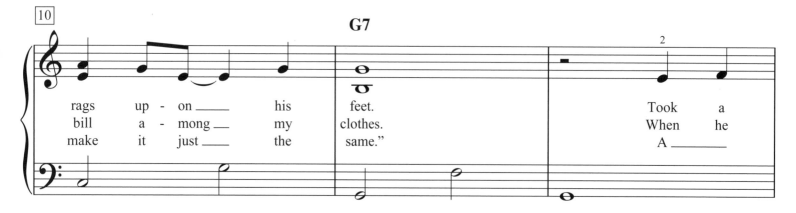

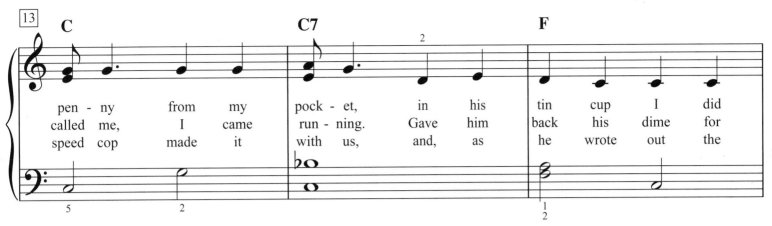

13 C / C7 / F

penny / from my / pocket, / in his
called me, / I came / running. / Gave him
speed cop / made it / with us, / and, as

tin / cup / I / did
back / his / dime / for
he / wrote / out / the

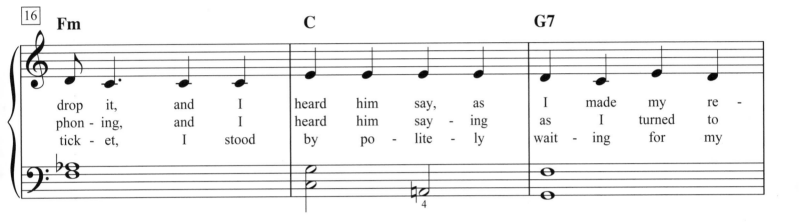

16 Fm / C / G7

drop it, / and I / heard / him / say, / as
phon-ing, / and I / heard / him / say-ing
tick-et, / I stood / by / po-lite-ly

I / made / my / re-
as / I / turned / to
wait-ing / for / my

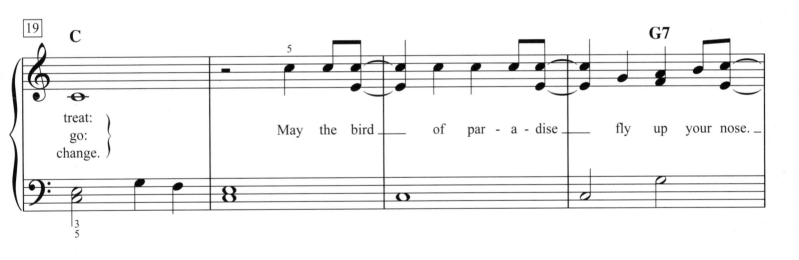

19 C / G7

treat:
go:
change.

May the bird / of par-a-dise / fly up your nose.

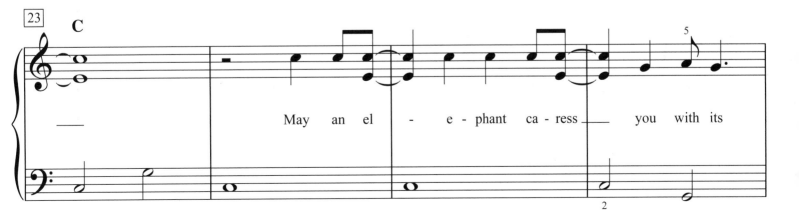

23 C

May an el- / e-phant ca-ress / you with its

toes. May your wife ___ be plagued with run-ners in her

hose. May the bird ___ of par-a-dise ___ fly up your nose.

1., 2. | 3.

My / I was

May the bird ___ of par-a-dise __

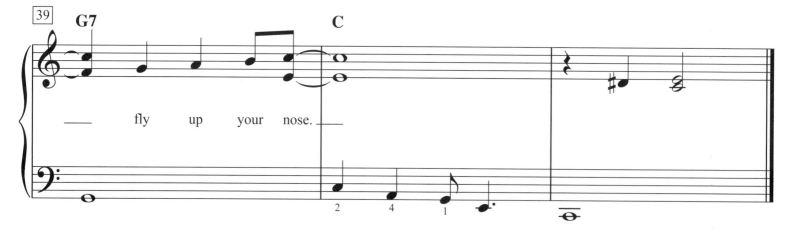

___ fly up your nose. ___

I WALK THE LINE

Words and Music by
JOHN R. CASH

Bright Country 2-beat

I keep a close watch on this heart of mine.
night is on dark and day is light,
close watch on this heart of mine.

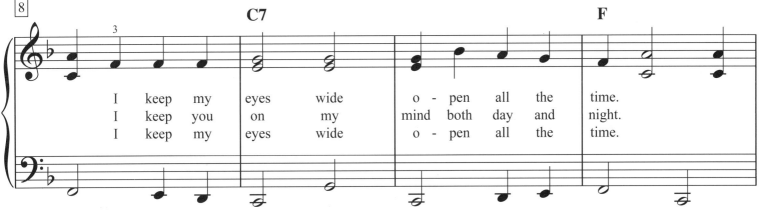

I keep my eyes wide o - pen all the time.
I keep you on my mind both day and night.
I keep my eyes wide o - pen all the time.

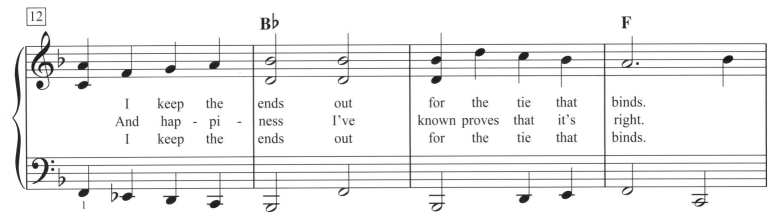

I keep the ends out for the tie that binds.
And hap - pi - ness I've known proves that it's right.
I keep the ends out for the tie that binds.

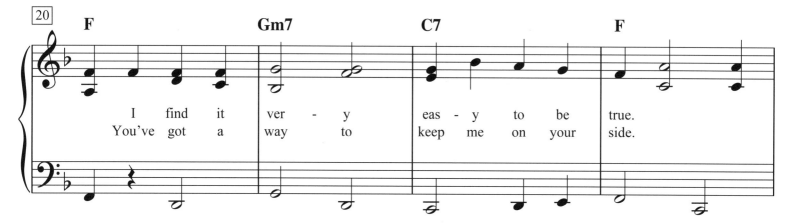

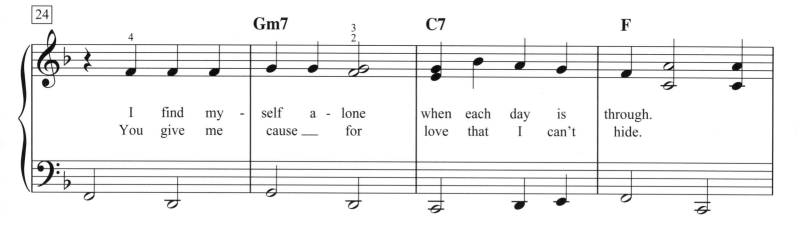

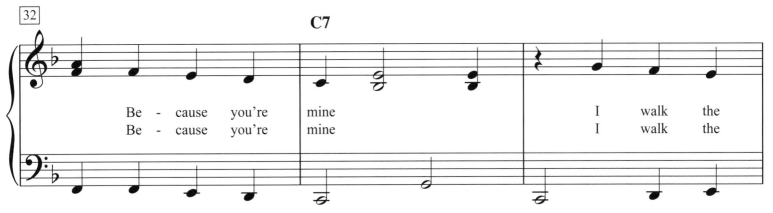

Be - cause you're mine
Be - cause you're mine
I walk the
I walk the

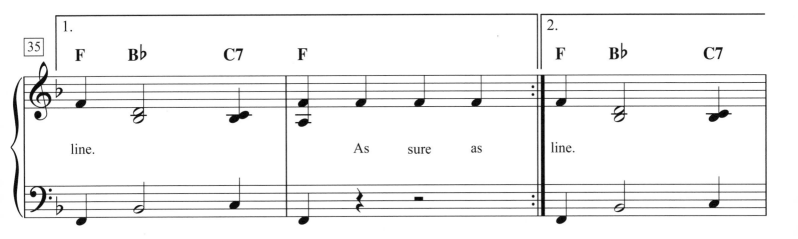

line.
As sure as
line.

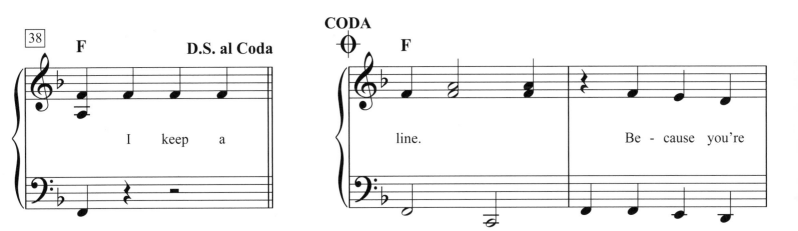

D.S. al Coda
I keep a

CODA
line.
Be - cause you're

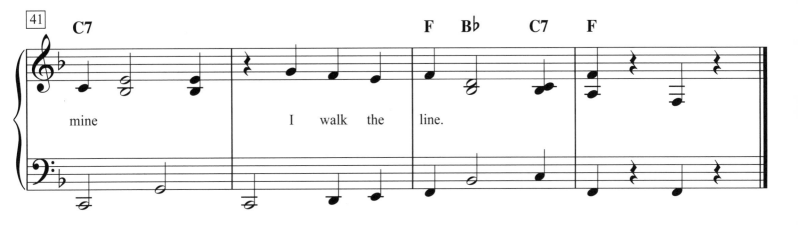

mine
I walk the line.

SIMPLE

Words and Music by MARK HOLMAN,
MICHAEL HARDY, TYLER HUBBARD
and BRIAN KELLEY

Happy Country feel, in 2

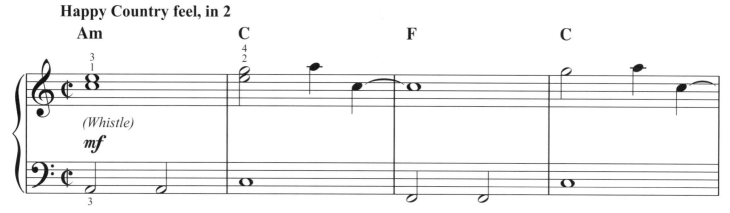

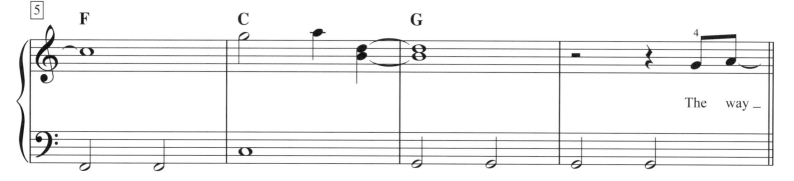

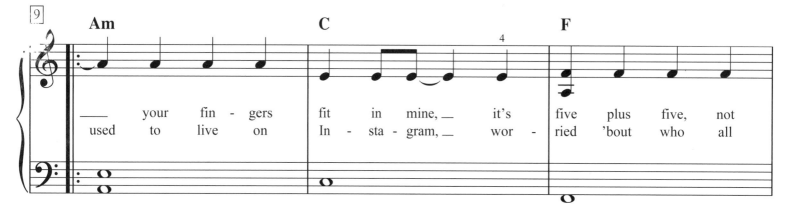

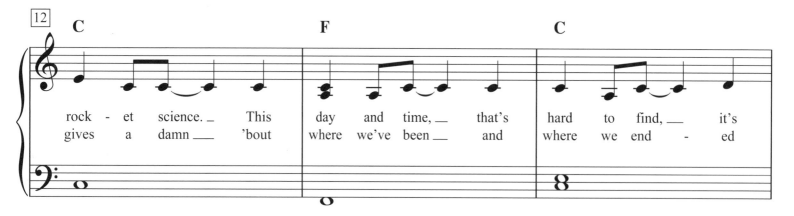

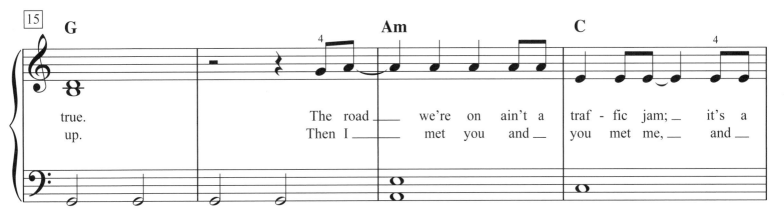

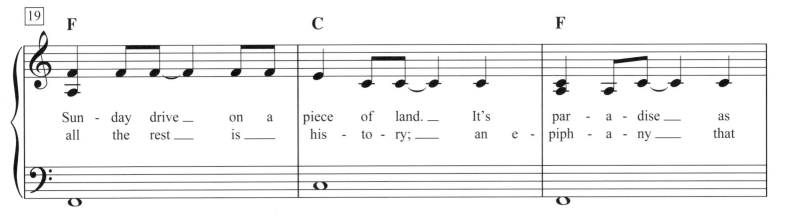

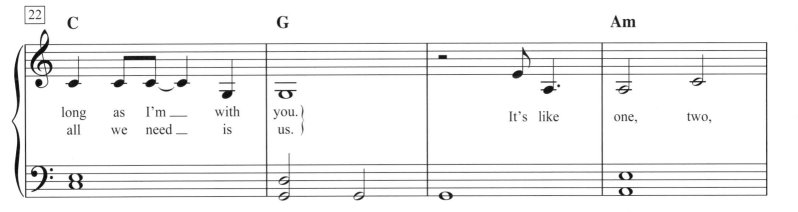

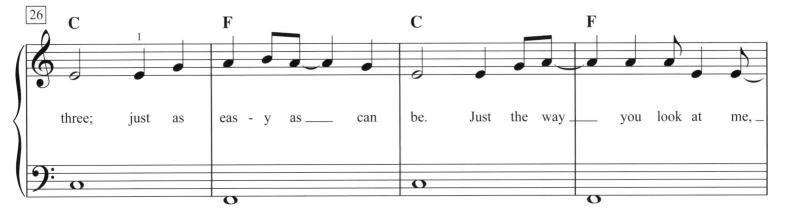

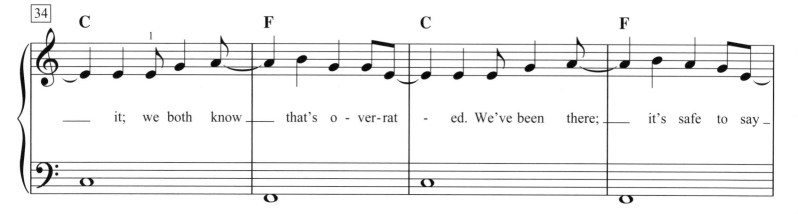

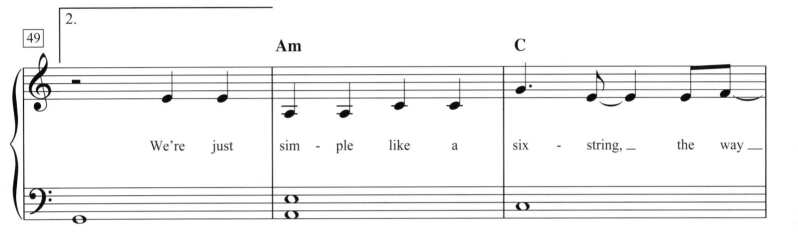

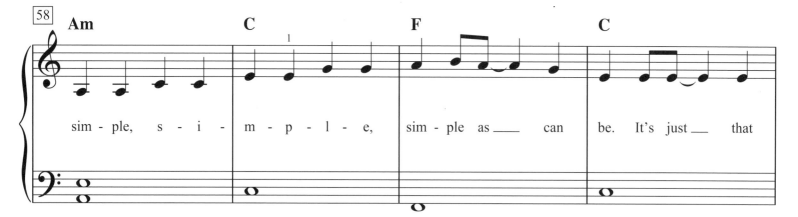

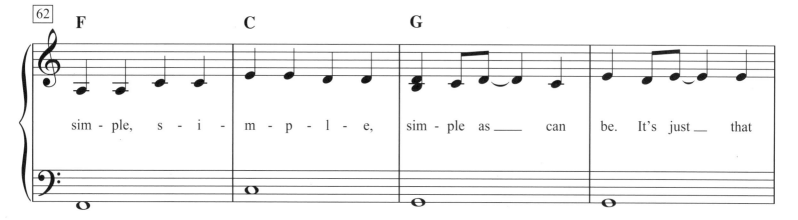

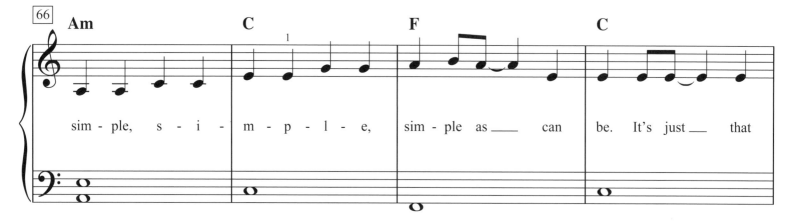

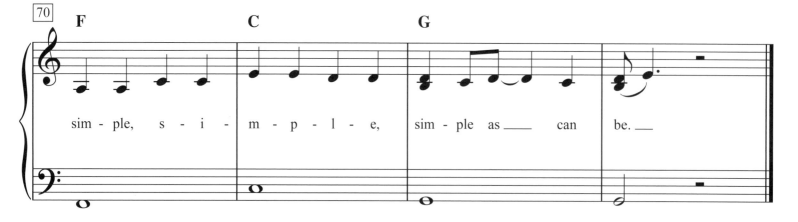

KEEP ON THE SUNNY SIDE

Words and Music by
A.P. CARTER

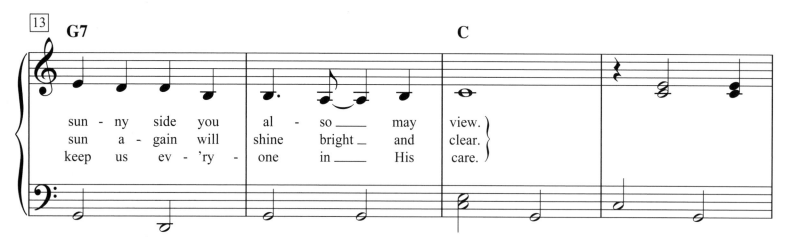

To Coda

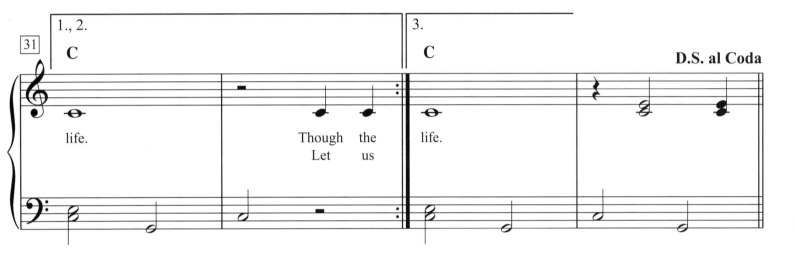

MOST PEOPLE ARE GOOD

Words and Music by JOSH KEAR,
DAVID FRASIER and EDWARD MONROE HILL

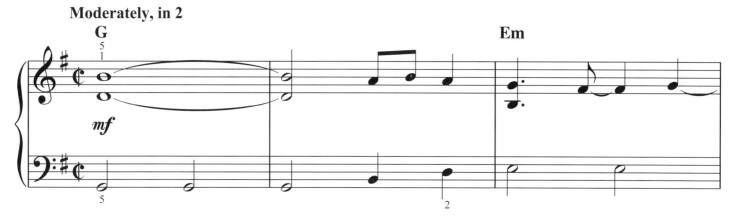

I be-lieve kids ought-a stay kids as long
I be-lieve them streets of gold are

___ as they can. ___
worth the work. ___ But Turn off the screen, go
I'd still ___ wan-na

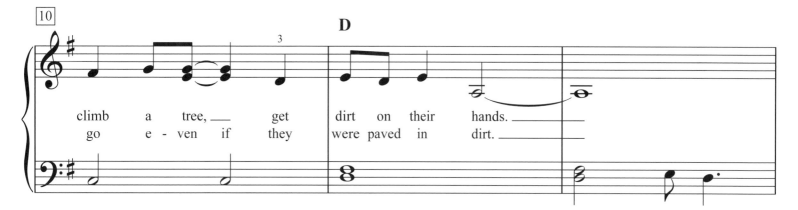

climb a tree, ___ get dirt on their hands. ___
go e-ven if they were paved in dirt. ___

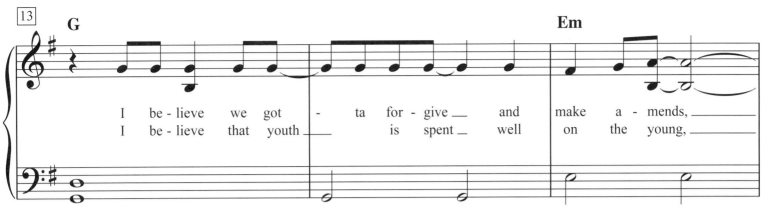

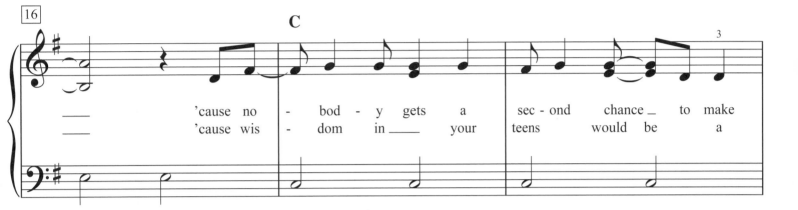

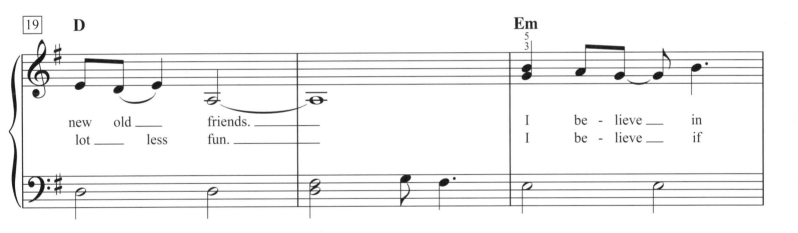

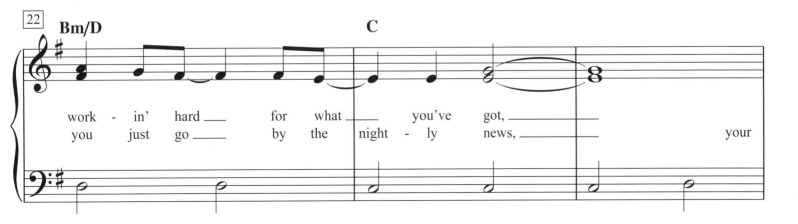

94

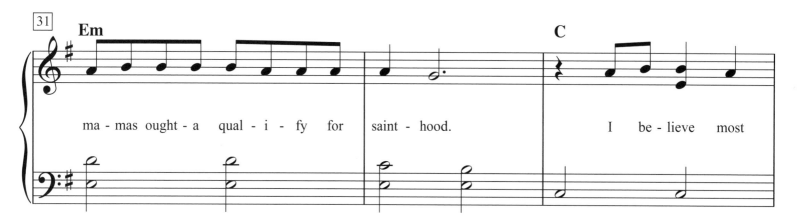

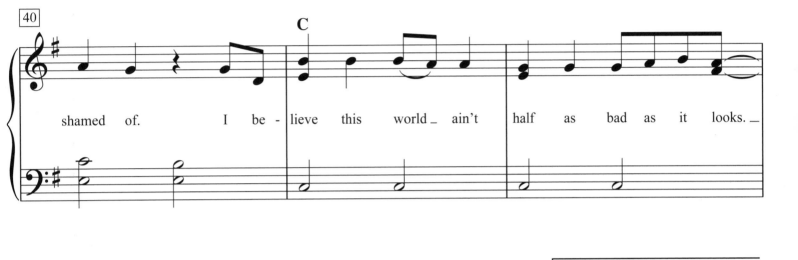

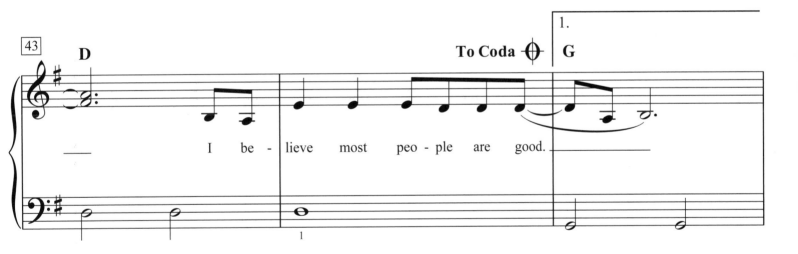

I be - lieve __ that days go slow and years __

__ go fast. __ And ev - 'ry breath's __ a

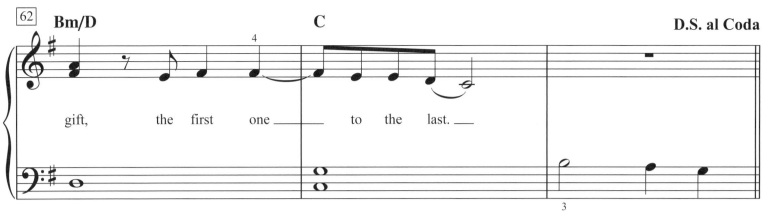

gift,   the first   one ____   to   the   last. ___

____   I   be -

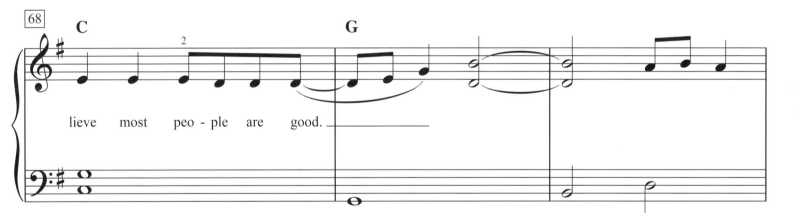

lieve   most   peo - ple   are   good. ____

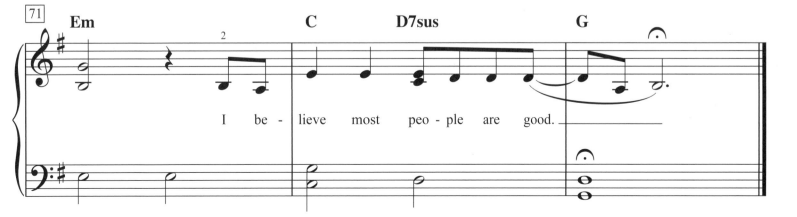

I   be - lieve   most   peo - ple   are   good. ___

SIXTEEN TONS

Words and Music by
MERLE TRAVIS

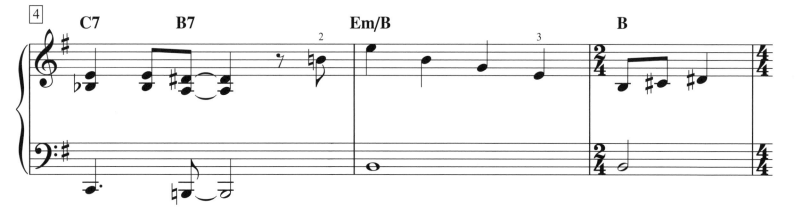

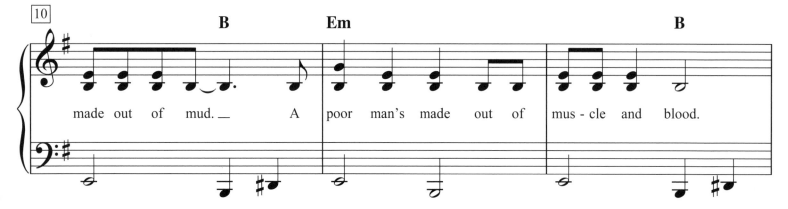

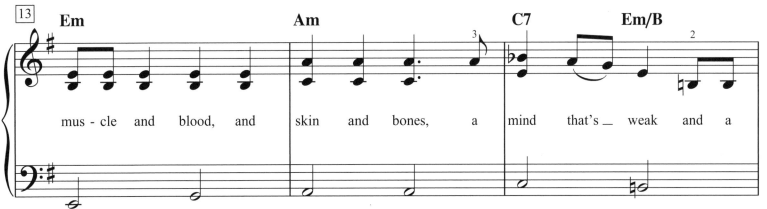

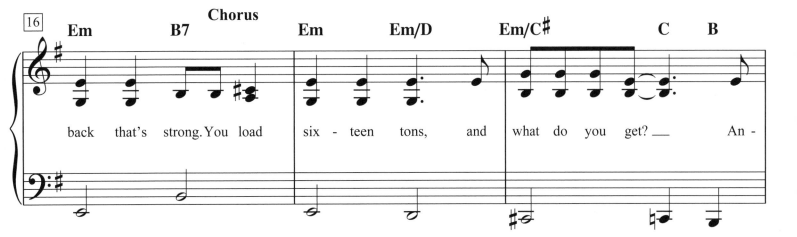

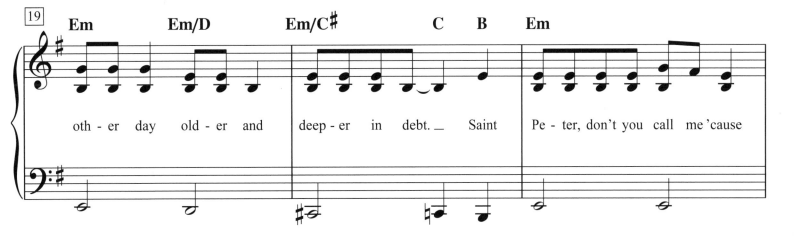

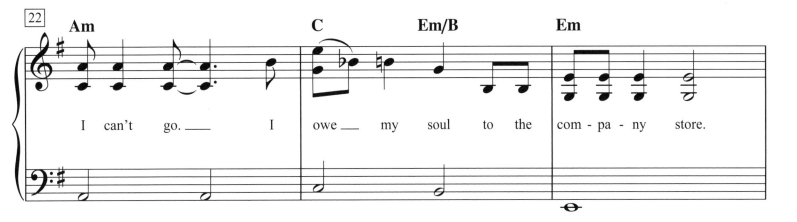

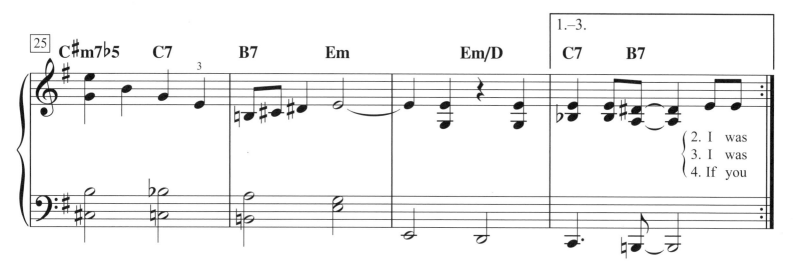

Additional Lyrics

2. I was born one mornin' when the sun didn't shine.
   I picked up my shovel and I walked to the mine.
   I loaded sixteen tons of number nine coal
   And the straw boss said, "Well-a bless my soul."
   Chorus

3. I was born one mornin', it was drizzling rain.
   Fightin' and trouble are my middle name.
   I was raised in a cane brake by an ole mama lion,
   Cain't no high-toned woman make me walk the line.
   Chorus

4. If you see me comin', better step aside.
   A lotta men didn't; a lotta men died.
   One fist of iron, the other of steel,
   If the right one don't a-get you, then the left one will.
   Chorus

RAINBOW

Words and Music by KACEY MUSGRAVES,
SHANE McANALLY and NATALIE HEMBY

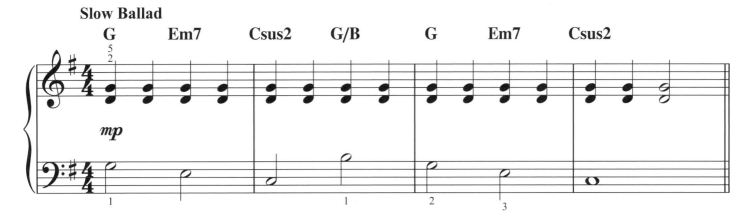

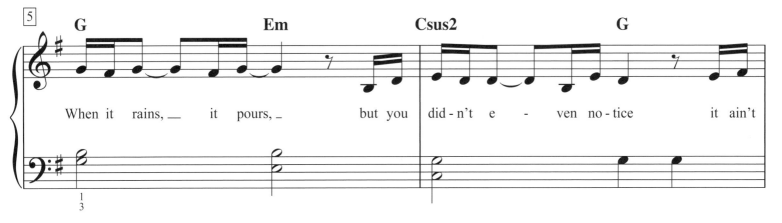

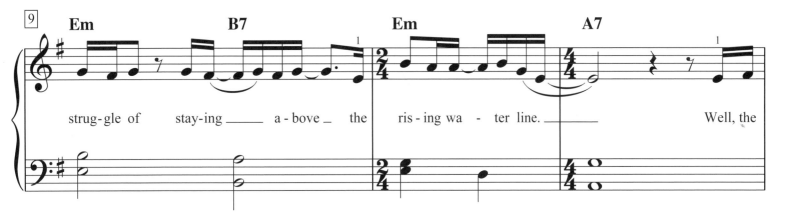

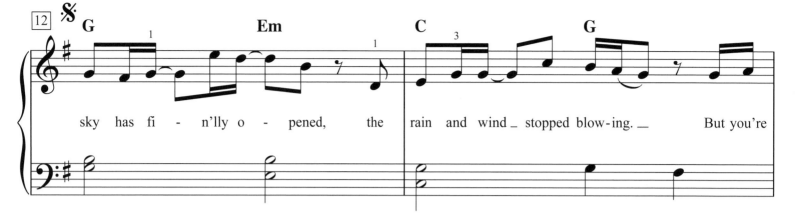

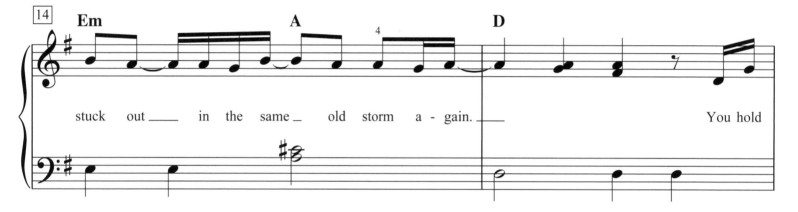

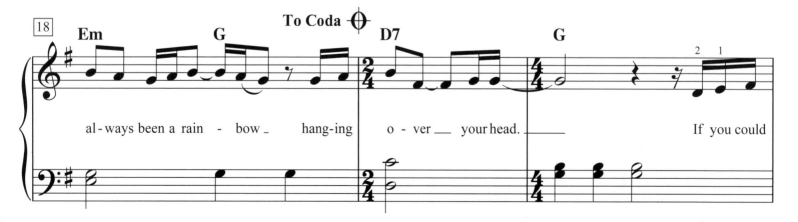

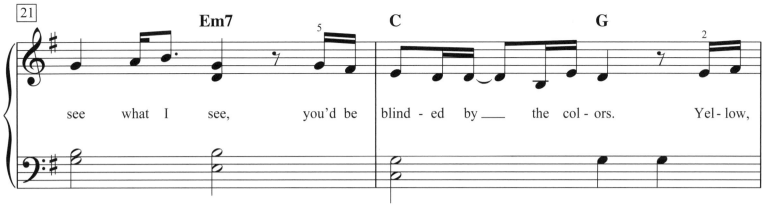

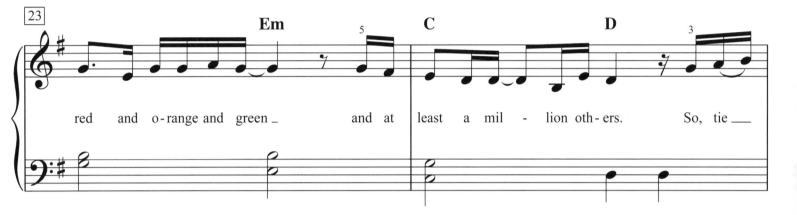

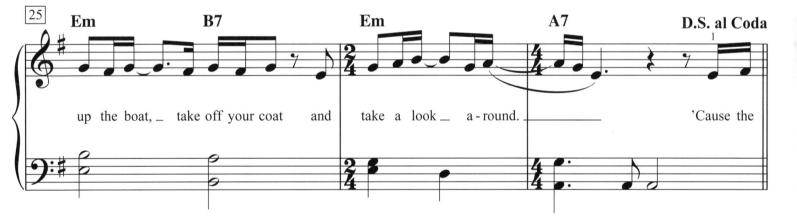

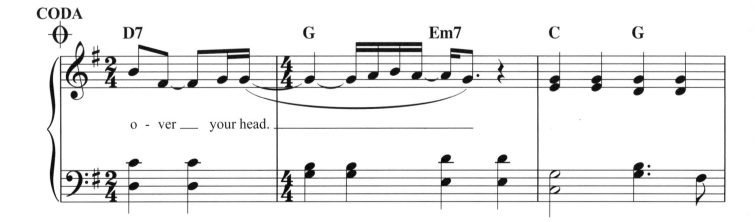

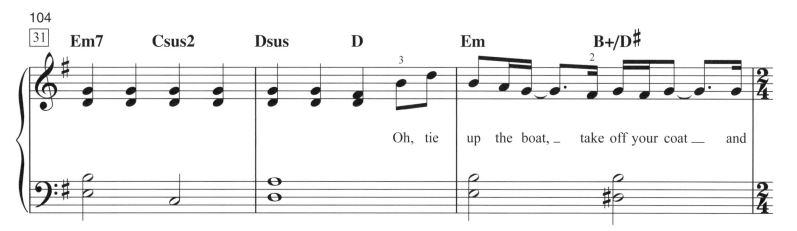

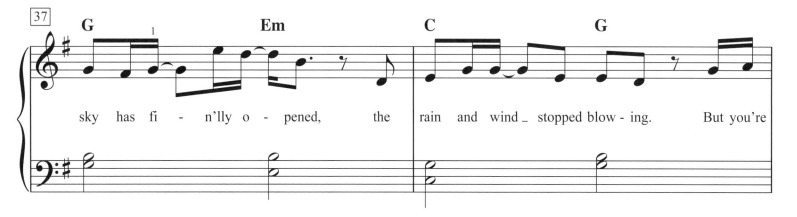

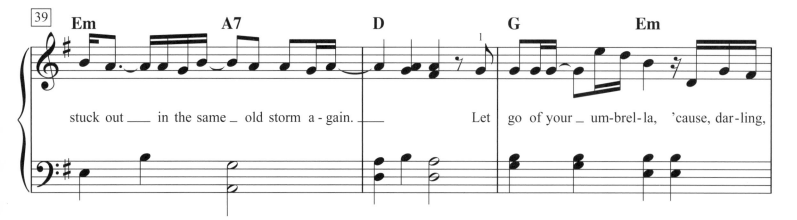

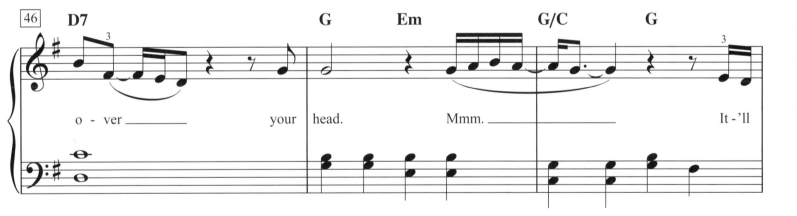

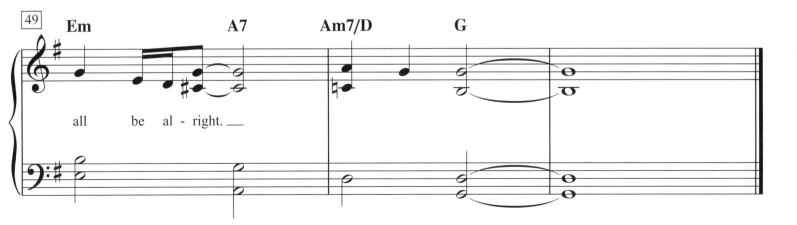

RING OF FIRE

Words and Music by MERLE KILGORE
and JUNE CARTER

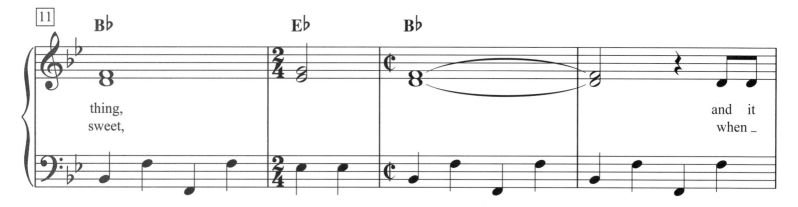

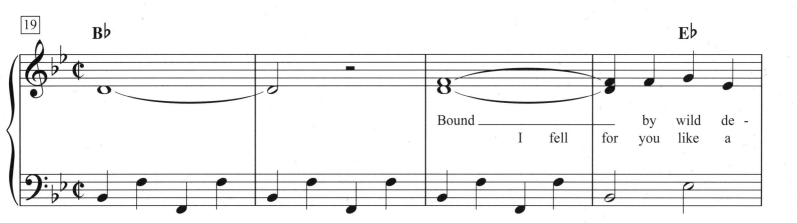

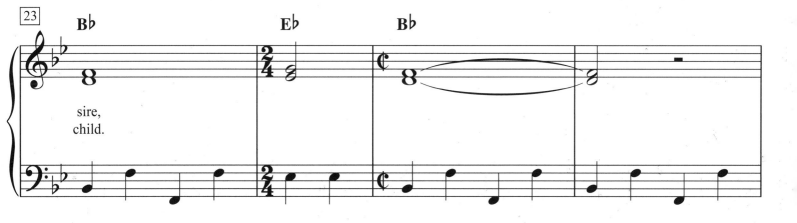

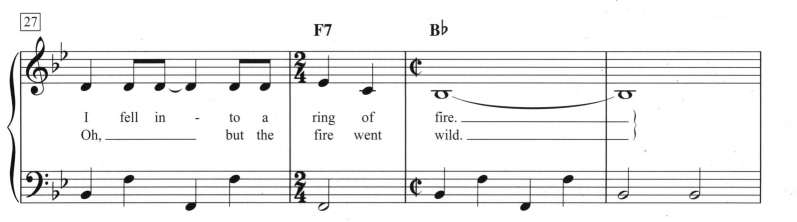

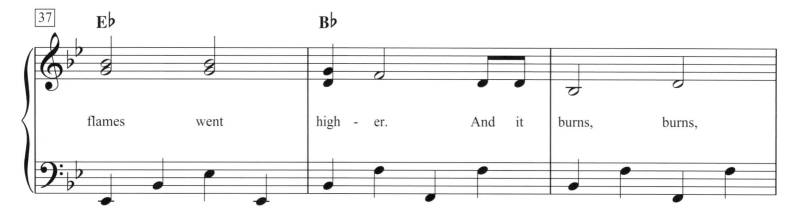

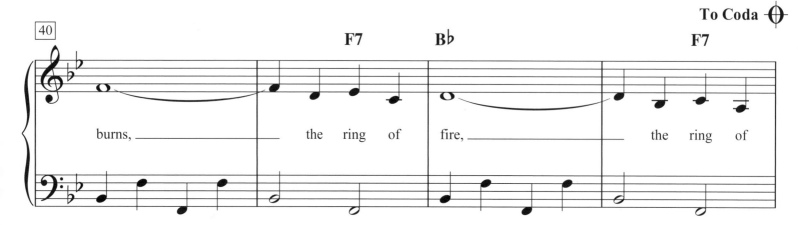

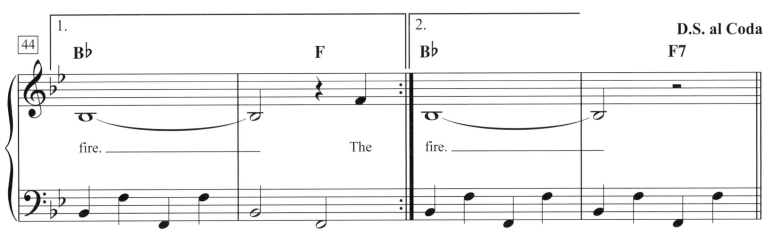

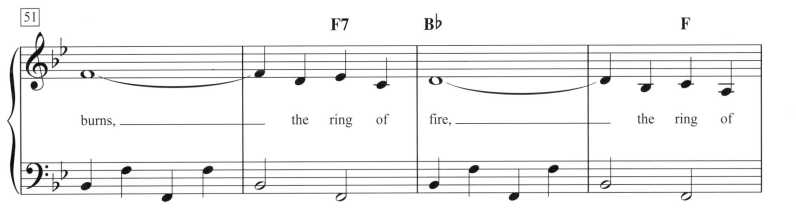

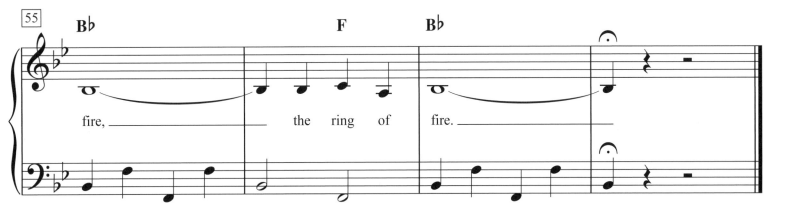

STUCK LIKE GLUE

Words and Music by KRISTIAN BUSH,
SHY CARTER, KEVIN GRIFFIN
and JENNIFER NETTLES

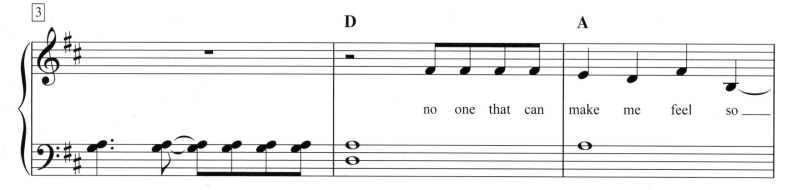

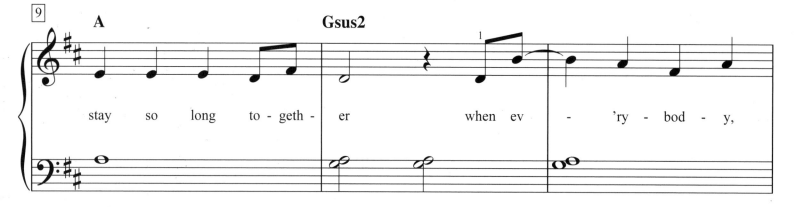

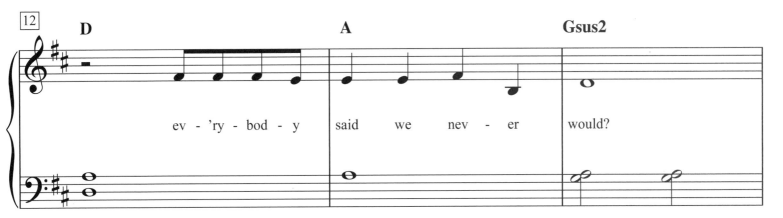

ev - 'ry - bod - y   said   we   nev - er   would?

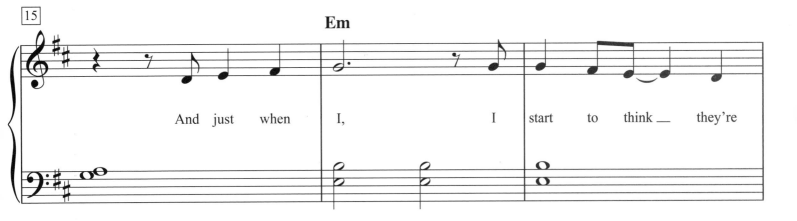

And   just   when   I,   I   start   to   think __   they're

right, __   that   love   has   died, __   there   you   go   mak - in'   my   heart __

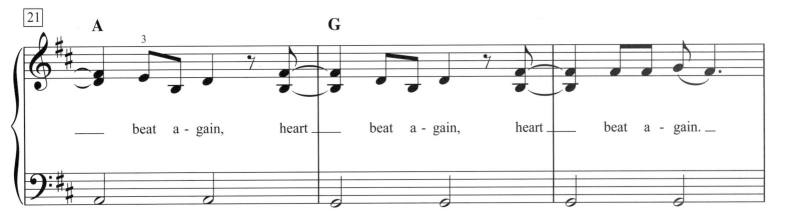

__   beat   a - gain,   heart __   beat   a - gain,   heart __   beat   a - gain. __

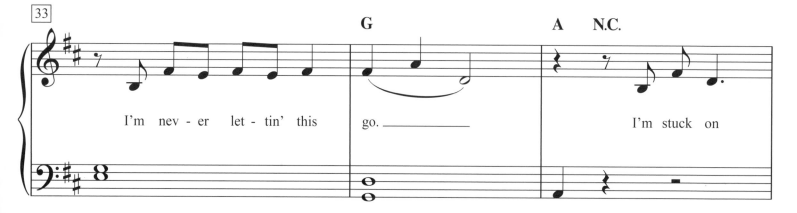

WIDE OPEN SPACES

Words and Music by
SUSAN GIBSON

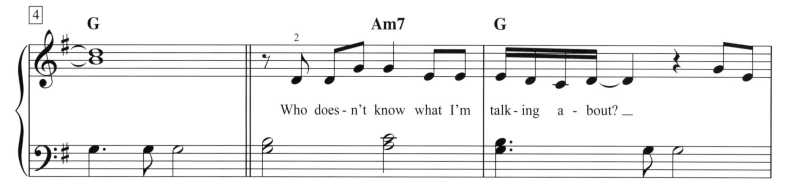

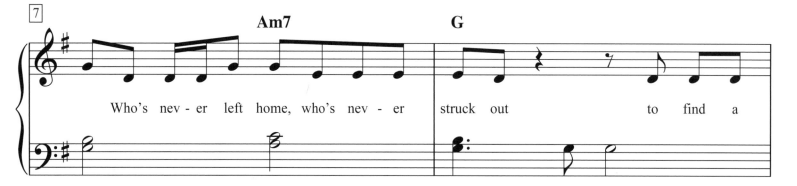

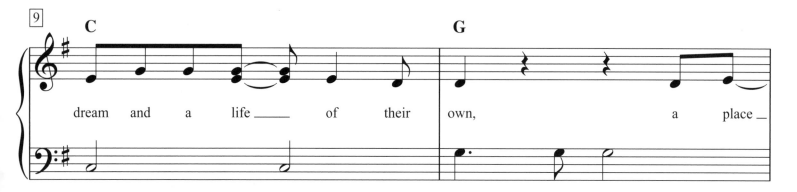

in the clouds, __ a foun - da - tion of stone? __

Man - y pre - cede and man - y will fol - low,
She trav - eled this road __ as __ a child, __

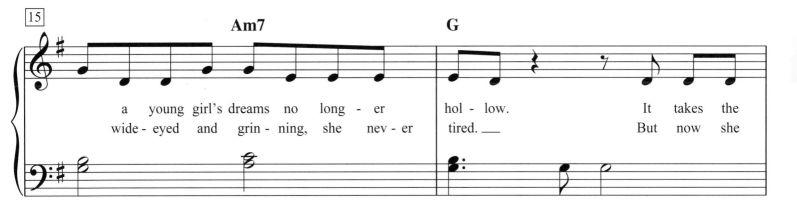

a young girl's dreams no long - er hol - low. It takes the
wide - eyed and grin - ning, she nev - er tired. __ But now she

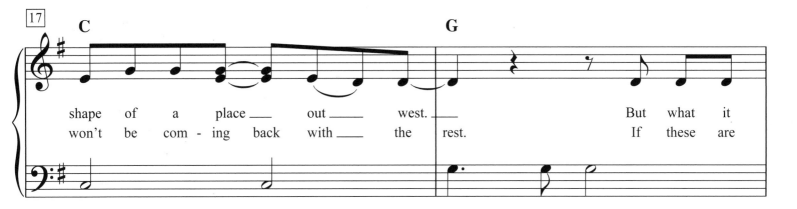

shape of a place __ out __ west. __ But what it
won't be com - ing back with __ the rest. If these are

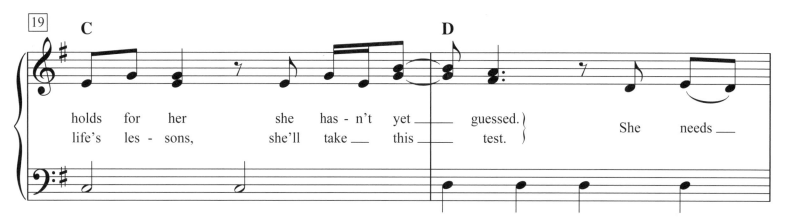

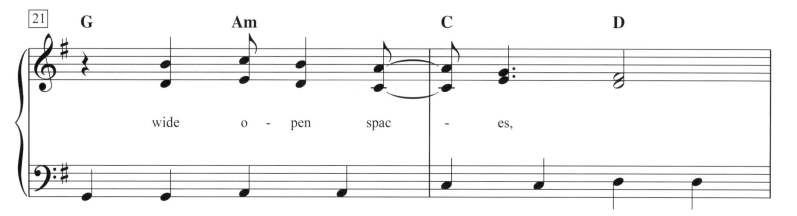

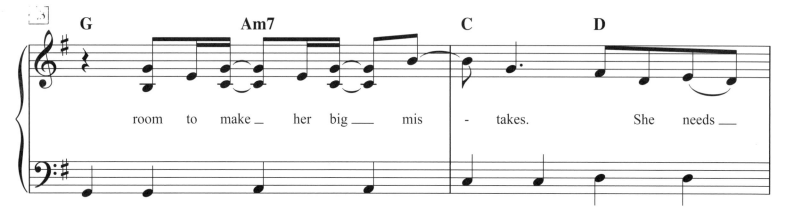

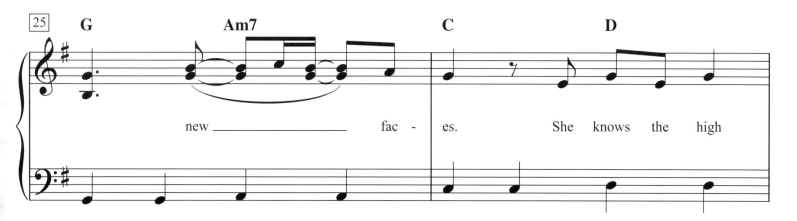

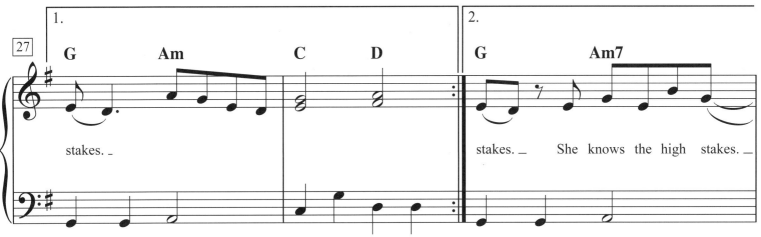

stakes. _   stakes. _ She knows the high stakes. _

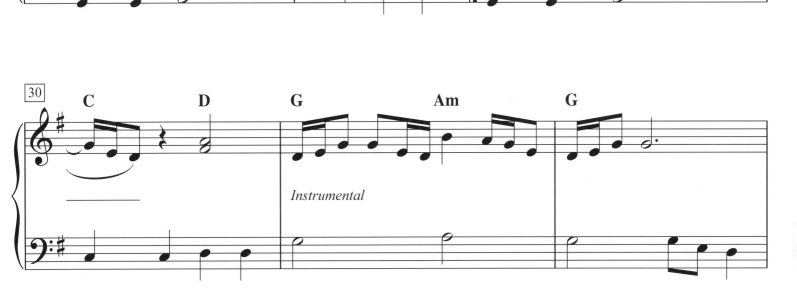

Instrumental

Instrumental ends

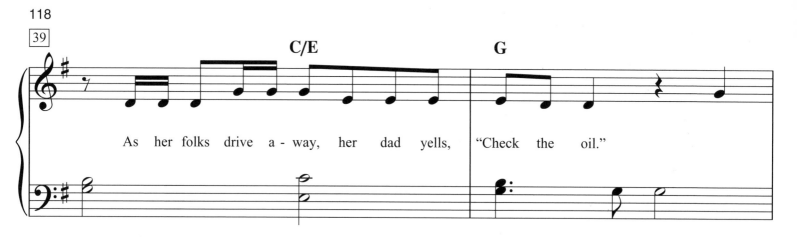

As her folks drive a-way, her dad yells, "Check the oil."

Mom stares out the win-dow and says, "I'm leav-in' my girl." She said, "It

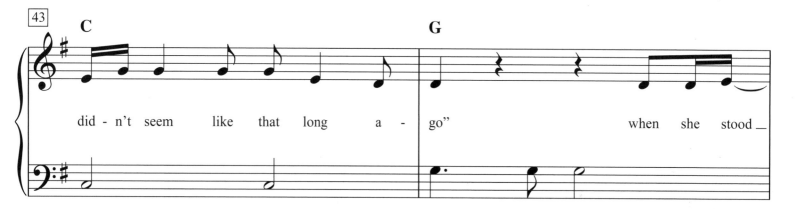

did-n't seem like that long a-go" when she stood __

__ there and let her own folks know __ she need-ed

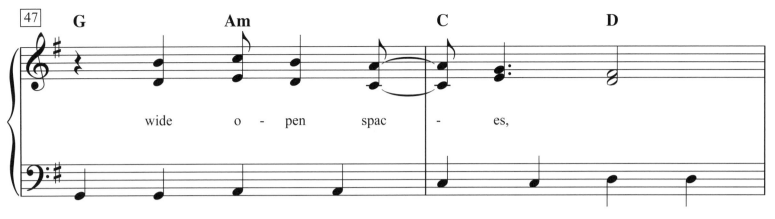

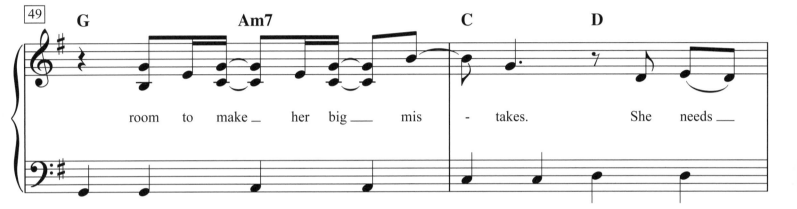

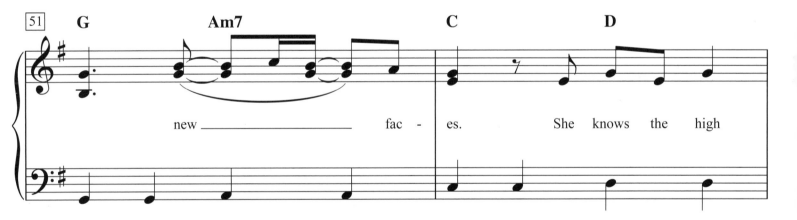

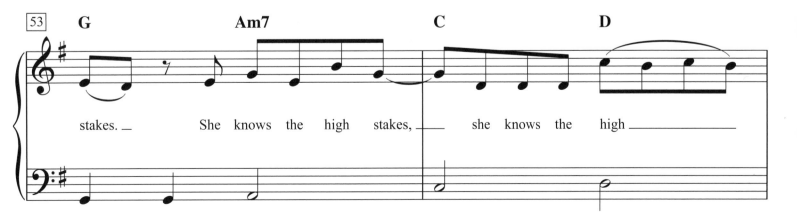

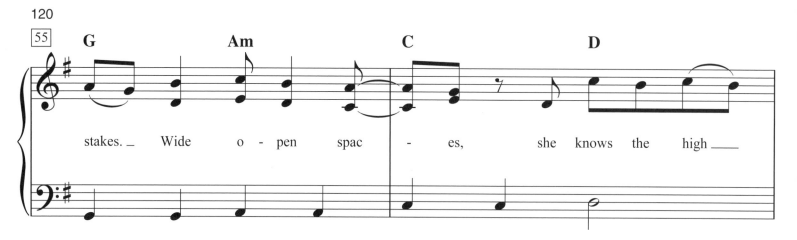

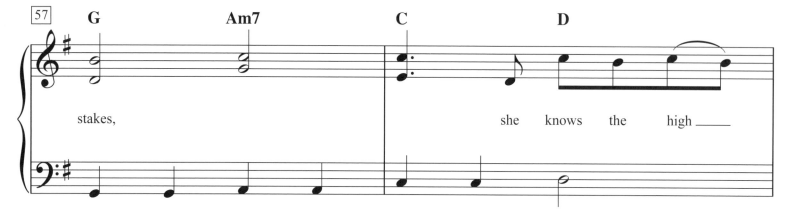

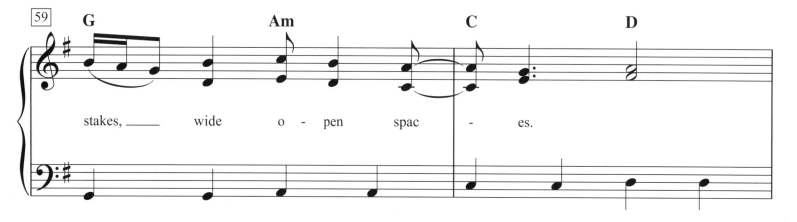

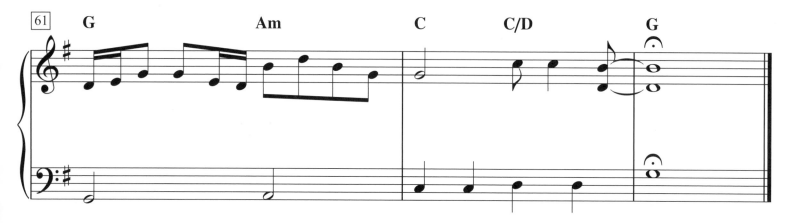